Choose to Flourish:
How to Change Career and Thrive in Life

By
RHIAN SHERRINGTON

Dedication

This book is dedicated to my twin sister Caryl. Without her by my side I'd be a shadow of who I am and hope still to be. Her love and expertise have kept me evolving and utterly supported. Here's to you kiddo!

For my children, Murray and Megan, my nieces Rowena and Elizabeth: I trust when your time comes, choosing to flourish comes with ease and much happiness.

For my husband, my rock, anchor and co-adventurer, still sailing away with me.

For my parents, your love and understanding mean the world.

Table of Contents

Dedication iii

About the Author vii

Acknowledgements ix
Client Confidentiality ix

Preface xi

A Few Helpful Pre-Conditions 1
External Change and Internal Transition – There's a Difference 2
Locus of Control 5
What's Your Viewpoint? 6
If Not Now, When? 7
    Signs that Say Time to Move On 7
    The 7-Year Cycle 9
    Seek Support 9
    Missing the Boat 10
Get Out Of Your Comfort Zone 12
    Avoid Panic, Work From Stretch 13

My Story 17

What is 'Flourishing'? 23
The Power of the Positive 26
Engagement, Meaning and Accomplishment in Work 29
    The Money Question 30
    Finding Our Meaning and Purpose 32
    Recognising Accomplishment 34
Positive Relationships 34

The Choose to Flourish Approach 39
Change Your Mind 42
Find Your Courage 43
Ditch the Sat Nav 45

Your Flourishing Map and Compass 46
Nurturing Resilience 48
Look After Your N-PALS 53
The 10 Steps 55

The Ten Steps to Successful Transition **59**
Step 1: Take Stock 59
Step 2: Let Go 63
Step 3: Know What You Need and Enjoy 65
Step 4: Find Your Strengths and Your Will 69
Step 5: Pin Point Your Location 73
Step 6: Identify A Destination 74
Step 7: Consistently Take Small Steps of Inspiring Action 76
Step 8: Actively Manage an Empowering Mind-Set 78
Step 9: Check Your Bearings 82
Step 10: Trust in Your New Beginning 86

Avoiding Common Pitfalls **89**
Illuminate the fears 89
Manage Your Energy (and Your Time) 91
Change and Other People 93
Immunity to Change: When You Can't Do What You Say You Will 97

Next Steps **101**
Tips and Hints 104
Your Invitation 106

Resources **109**

About the Author

Rhian Sherrington is an Executive and Confident Transitions Coach based in Bristol, UK. Her passion is enabling others to thrive in careers that feed their soul as well as their bank balance.

Her 'Choose2Flourish' Programme takes the anxiety and stress out of changing career direction, whether that's stepping up into leadership or seeking new purpose and meaning. Rhian understands from personal experience, and that of her clients, that following your heart to a flourishing life needs more than just wishful thinking. It requires courage, self-belief and confidence, the guiding principles in her Choose2Flourish Approach and 10-Step guide outlined here.

An avid learner, Rhian holds a degree in Geography from Oxford University, a Masters degree in Environmental Management and further Diplomas in Training & Development, Personal Performance Coaching and Executive & Corporate Coaching. Her previous book, **'Alchemy for the Mind: Create Your Confident Core'** has enjoyed 5 star reviews on Amazon. She enjoys keeping up to date with change leadership, neuroscience and positive psychology to inform her coaching programmes. She loves Qi Gong, surfing, family cycling and walking adventures, especially when they involve picnics in wild and beautiful places.

Canningford House
1st Floor
38 Victoria Street
Bristol
BS1 6BY

Acknowledgements

My sincere gratitude goes to all my wonderful clients who have trusted me to assist them on their journeys. Your courage and determination has been inspiring. Thanks again to Chris Sherrington, for his superb editing skills and quality assurance on my use of the English language. And thanks to Patrick and Marie Dahdal for their support and expertise in getting this book into publication.

Client Confidentiality

All clients mentioned in this book have had their names changed in order to protect coach-client confidentiality.

Preface

Happiness is not something you postpone for the future:
It is something you design for the present.

Zig Zaglar

Does a different future beckon to you?

Do you feel an inner yearning that is difficult to identify and even harder to put into words? Does it call out to you to look again at where you are heading? Or is there so much frustration with where you are now that you'd down tools tomorrow – if only you knew what to do, where you could go?

If any of that resonates with you, then this book is for you.

This isn't a book about how to craft an attractive LinkedIn profile (though it's likely you'll need one at some point). We're not going into how to approach and work with recruitment agencies, write the best personal statement or resumé. This book doesn't consider psychological surveys that match your attributes to job roles.

What this book *is* going to do is lead you through the minefield of inner transformation that is required when you realise you need to do something different with your life but don't know what that is or how you're going to get there. We're going to walk hand in hand through my 'Choose to Flourish' approach so that you CAN transition into a new job role, new sector or career with complete confidence and assurance of where you are going and why you are going there. From that, you can best work out the 'how', setting yourself clear, simple steps to move forwards.

We look at you 'in the round', making sure you're equipped with the best tools to find your way. After all, life is a journey and if you want to be the one who is truly exploring it, you'd better make sure you've got your map and compass – not some sub-standard, unreliable sat nav that'll take you off course and up some narrow road to a dead end.

So, come on in and let's get started!

CHAPTER 1

A Few Helpful Pre-Conditions

Realise you are responsible for your life. The decisions, the choices you make are yours. Don't blame others for things not working out, take responsibility, change the things that need changing.

So you need change. You don't like your work – it's lost its allure. The passion that was once there has faded. Perhaps change has found you - doesn't it find everyone at some point? - maybe through an organisational restructure resulting in redundancy or a new role. You may have survived a personal experience that has shifted your foundations. Bereavement, divorce, illness, a near-death experience or a shift in how you view the world – these all bring change to us. Or it could be something less dramatic, something unstoppable but stealthy. It may move so slowly that you barely acknowledge it in your life until one day, the force of its presence smacks right into you. Yes, you got older. Your previous lens on life has been removed and a new one is slowly being slotted into place. With your own mortality becoming more tangible, the big questions need to be answered, such as 'what am I *doing* with my life?'

Often when we've been through a change event we can think that it's all done. We've survived and are now 'over it'. There is, however, a vital need to 'catch up with ourselves'. We need to acknowledge and work with an *inner* transformation, the internal process of **transition**. It is this internal transition that will enable us to move from where we currently are to where we want to be. This is true whether change has happened to you, whether you are the one driving through that change or whether you are now responding to the natural process of moving through a key life stage as you age. The first 'pre-condition' of successfully navigating a career change is therefore, to understand that whilst the change we may be looking for in our career is something *external*, we fully need to be aware of the *internal transition process.*

So many people fail at this first hurdle, as they want to launch themselves wholeheartedly into the next 'new' thing, whether that's the new job, partner or place to live. You will waste considerable time, energy and probably money if you don't stop and consider what is really going on. We can't prevent change happening to us (and most of us wouldn't really want to) but you can put yourself in a far stronger place to manage that process, enabling yourself to thrive in your career and other aspects of your life.

Hopefully this has caught your attention and you're ready to read on. Let's first of all examine in some detail this process of 'transition'.

External Change and Internal Transition – There's a Difference

In Western Culture many of us have lost the realisation that we go through many phases of transition in life. We may talk about 'being in transition', but often without fully appreciating the depth of the process.

Whilst an external change, (such as divorce, redundancy, bereavement or a new job) may trigger a transition, transition itself is something altogether more profound, an *internal* experience. Transition is the psychological process we go through as we adapt internally to things such as having a baby, buying a new house or getting married. Organisational change programmes now recognise the importance of dealing with this internal process of transition and not just hoping leaders and managers will 'make it happen' as perhaps they were more often expected to in the past.

It's important to acknowledge that we should all expect a lifetime of transitions as we move through the *ageing process*. As a society we make light of the 'mid-life' crisis that may hit at 40 or 50, but it's a truth that the '0's do often signify important shifts in our outlook on life and our place in the scheme of things. Even if nothing significant appears to have happened from an external perspective, those experiencing such a shift may be feeling adrift and rudderless as what used to give that satisfying buzz now leaves them empty. Given that we all age, it's a shame that so many of us are ill prepared for what is essentially a natural and somewhat inevitable process.

William Bridges, in his book 'Transitions: Making Sense of Life's Changes' helpfully points out that we need to be aware of the 3 stages to transition if we are to successfully navigate ourselves through this process, coming out the other side stronger and clearer:

1. The Ending - when we feel disengaged, disorientated and disenchanted. Here we must recognise what we need to **let go** of. It could be things that no longer fit 'who' we are, whether that be our assumptions, ways of thinking or behaviours. It's important that we spend time acknowledging what we have *lost*. For example, the sense of loss around no longer having the same level of purpose and motivation in your work; the loss of old work colleagues, or feeling comfortable with how you used to do things in your previous role. In becoming a parent, there is the loss of your old freedoms. There could be feelings of both anxiety (how can I cope?) and happiness (that at last, things are changing). Acknowledging both our loss and what we need to let go of creates a powerful and necessary shift in our conscious and subconscious in the transition process.

2. **The Neutral Zone** – a place of emptiness, confusion and false starts. This is when the old way of doing things has been rejected but a new way has yet to found. Everything here feels in a state of

flux and you don't know what you're doing. The neutral zone feels uncomfortable and we may wish to rush through it, to jump onto the first new thing that comes by but it's essential we sit with the discomfort. We need to find time to be alone and let things 'just be' for a while as our unconscious mind processes and assimilates. It is normal to move through a range of feelings that might include anger, fear, guilt, depression, possible denial and disillusionment. You might feel that you are procrastinating and unable to make decisions, or you make a decision only to quickly return back to question it again and again. Circular thoughts patterns can be common and focus, clarity and self-confidence can be noticeably lacking.

3. **The New Beginning** - only after moving through the ending and the neutral zone can we expect a new beginning. It may appear as a hunch, a dream, a fluttery idea whose time has now come. Trust your feelings and be confident that when you are ready for the new beginning, an opportunity will come. The new beginning feels 'right', comfortable, the only way. Gradual acceptance builds up, including greater self-efficacy and more positive feelings that "I can do this". Getting to this point, you can feel 'lighter', like a load has been taken off your shoulders. Decision-making gets easier as you grow in confidence, have clarity and can focus on your path.

Whatever the cause of change, whether it's because you're getting older and feeling your mortality for the first time, or because an external event as triggered something in you or for you, we all go through these phases of transition as a response. The only difference between us is the *speed* at which we move through the phases. A whole variety of factors can combine to influence this rate of movement. For example, your past experiences, your preferred way of doing things and whether change was foisted upon you.

So before you start to throw yourself into the next 'new thing' – stop!

If you are feeling you're 'in transition', identifying *where you are in terms of these three stages* is essential for you to not only 'survive' transition, but to flourish. This is one of the helpful 'pre-conditions' to success.

Locus of Control

Some people really struggle with change, whilst for others its' like water off a duck's back. One important factor at work here seems to be the **locus of control**. A concept developed by Julian B Rotter in the field of personality psychology, locus of control refers to the extent to which you believe you are in control of what happens to you and what happens in your life.

People with a high **internal locus of control** will find they often cope well with change, believing their actions can lead to positive outcomes for them. When you've got a high internal locus of control, you believe that your attributes, hard work and decisions will ensure your success. You make things happen; you control your destiny.

Those with a high **external** locus of control tend to become very stressed by change as they believe they have little or no control over the outcomes. Here you are at the mercy of others, of 'fate' or luck, independent from your attributes, hard work or decisions. Things happen to you - 'they' control your destiny.

Being aware of where you are in terms of your locus of control can provide powerful insights for transitioning into a new career. You can discover your locus of control by coming to my website and doing a simple quiz – visit www.choose2flourish.co.uk/lcquiz.

Having a higher internal locus of control is very helpful when you are in a career transition as it enables you to believe you can take control. It empowers you to do something about the frustrations or difficulties

— 5 —

you may be facing. We'll come back to this important aspect as part of the '10 Steps' in Chapter 5.

What's Your Viewpoint?

Your 'locus of control' is an important shaper of your viewpoint. Are you a protagonist or a victim? How much choice do you think you have over your career? The late Stephen R Covey, a leading figure in personal development, concluded after decades of research that 10% of what happens to us, we have no control over, leaving 90% that we can control. One way in which we do have control is that we can **choose** how we think, respond and act to whatever is going on around us. If you have a high external locus of control, you're going to find that statement difficult to swallow, but do bear with me – it's all about working out how you can create that space, and belief, that you can choose.

On question I often ask my groups is this: "What if you were the hero or heroine in your life, your story – what would you expect to happen?" The answers that invariably come back lead to one main conclusion – we'd expect to succeed, we'd have hope and self-belief. Things may get very challenging, practically impossible, but the hero/heroine persists, digs deep inside and manages to pull through. Often there are significant others who provide help and support along the way (who ever said we have to do this stuff alone?), but it is the hero/ heroine who finds what is needed inside themselves to make it happen.

Another aspect that is helpful to reflect on at this stage is this: Are you operating in a vacuum or can you tap into something larger to guide your way? One of the most profound questions Albert Einstein pondered was whether or not the Universe was friendly. He concluded yes. Whether or not you are religious, believe in God, have a spiritual belief system or are led by a belief in the goodness of humanity, I would whole-heartedly encourage you to take Einstein's example and believe the Universe means you well. When you can reach outside of yourself and find an external source to connect to, some of the weight of trying to change direction, of seeking a new, more fulfilling path falls away.

If Not Now, When?

Wouldn't it be so straightforward if we could just recognise when we've outlived our current job and need to move on? That another future is waiting there for us – *right now*! Another important pre-condition to a successful career transition is to recognise that there may never be a 'perfect time'. We can get stalled in the 'neutral zone' of transition if we fail to recognise this and seek out solutions that are 100% risk free or perfect. Understanding what you need to make a decision is important here. If you find yourself procrastinating, it's usually a sign that you lack clarity around what you are looking for. There could also be an underlying, subconscious fear that has you in its grip, sabotaging your efforts.

Signs that Say Time to Move On

Clients who have just started to work with me often say the following;

"I don't feel passionate about what I do anymore"

"I'm getting demoralised about my performance. I don't seem to have the same impact I used to have and that's affecting my confidence".

"I feel stuck and exhausted. I've got plans but I never seem to have the energy to do anything about them"

"I know I'm fearful around what I'd really like to do. This is making me procrastinate more and more – I can't seem to make myself take any action"

"I just don't know what I can do. I hate myself for staying here where I'm so unhappy but as I can't see myself doing something different or being elsewhere, I'm resigned to making do'.

It's not always easy to know you are on the wrong path. It often starts with a niggling feeling that won't go away, despite your efforts to ignore it. Paulo Coelho in his book 'The Alchemist' talks about how it is your heart that gives you the feedback that you're on the right path or not. Learning to listen, and to trust, your heart, keeps you aligned to your unique purpose in life. According to 'The Alchemist' our purpose is what we have always desired; it is something we have always wanted to do or be. Navigating your way through a change in career requires a sensitive integration of heart and mind; of listening to your feelings as well as your reasoning. Learning to tune into and use your intuition, your 'gut instinct' is also vital.

How we experience the signs it's time to move on varies but common features include:

➢ You are dulled by the routine;

➢ There is no longer any sense of accomplishment;

➢ You feel detached from the vision, values or challenges of the organisation or business;

➢ Everything is too easy – you are bored;

➢ An increase in the frequency and intensity of feelings of frustration, irritability and possibly anger. Sometimes these feelings cannot be contained at work but seep out, negatively impacting your personal life.

➢ No longer feeling valued in your role, perhaps a sense you are being overlooked or that you have been 'pigeon-holed' in some way.

As the previous description of the neutral zone outlined, the time before we are ready for the next thing is very confusing. We can suffer from low moods and we run the risk of being depressed. Feeling detached and lacking in energy is perhaps to be expected but if your symptoms get very intense and you don't feel any improvement in your mood over a few weeks, do go and seek professional medical help. One in 9 adults experience a bout of depression at least once in their life and it's very important to get proper support.

The 7-Year Cycle

Give or take 1 or 2 years, there is a 7-year cycle where we shift from seeking novelty in our work to seeking mastery. Looking back at your major career and role changes to date will give you an idea of where you might be in this cycle. Have you missed a turn of the cycle? Are you due a shift back into novelty? Understanding where you are in this cycle is tremendously helpful when you start to actively seek change in your career. Occasionally we can react to difficulties in our life by running away – the 'flight' reaction in response to perceived and real threat. When you seek to move on in your career, you should be clear that you are *choosing* to do this and not *acting out patterns of behaviour* and *reacting* in ways that aren't serving you.

Seek Support

Recognising the signs that it's time for a new direction or role, and then *acting on* them is not an easy matter. If you've been struggling with this for some time, please be reassured. Whilst some people may appear to confidently and successfully jump from one thing into another, that doesn't mean to say they've found it easy. I suspect some of my friends and acquaintances think my switch from Senior Manager in a charity into running my own successful coaching business has been a breeze. 'It's alright for you, you <insert whatever special attribute that person thinks you have and they haven't>."

Like most people in such situations, I haven't necessarily shared the details of the process I've been going through with my nearest and dearest. My coach knows though, along with a small circle of like-minded peers and friends who having been going through similar transformation. Seeking out help and support is vital. Even when I wasn't sure how I could cover the cost, I've sought out professional guidance, as I know becoming an 'overnight success' takes many months, possibly years, of inner transformation and mastery over your mind-set and subsequent control and direction of your actions. Without this support, the answer to this 'if not now, when?' question can easily become 'never'. One pre-condition of a successful transition, therefore, is knowing who you have in your life that can support you, and seeking out that assistance if it's currently missing.

Missing the Boat

One of the reasons people end up getting, and remaining, stuck is that it can be easy to miss the signs described previously that tell us it's time to go. Common reasons for doing so include:

- ➤ We're so caught up in the busy-ness of the day to day we forget to stop, breathe and check in with what is *really* going on around us;

- ➤ We have no clue, no vision about what to do next;

- ➤ We like things to feel safe, secure and stable and the idea of change frightens us as we have a low tolerance of risk;

- ➤ The weight of our responsibilities prevents us from allowing ourselves to even *think* of other possibilities, let alone take any action;

- ➤ We've got negative thoughts and beliefs running inside our heads that over-ride any yearning for anything new. Key ways in which these negative thoughts get expressed are;

  - o Not being good enough;

  - o Being too old (too young) to change;

o   Having to be grateful for what we've got;

o   Feeling it's not the 'done thing' to expect more;

o   Haven't got the money/time;

o   Not being confident enough.

Repetition of such thoughts creates beliefs about ourselves, around what we can and cannot do. They become 'storylines' which can act as an internal saboteur, preventing us from moving successfully through the transition process and into a new role or career. It is essential that we identify and challenge such beliefs, and that requires examining our mind-set.

Guilt can often be the hidden factor behind some of these negative belief patterns. Feeling guilty can prevent us from listening to the signs we should be doing something different. For example, if we're currently in a role that we know many other people would give their right arm to be doing, the guilty feelings can stall any further exploration of other feelings that are suggesting it's time we moved on. Perhaps we've invested lots of time and money into gaining qualifications for a specific vocation but once in it, we realise it's not for us. For example, it takes courage, once significant investments have been made, to step back from being a doctor, architect or lawyer.

We may get a longed for promotion and then realise it's actually not what we want at all. I remember feeling over the moon after being told I'd got a Senior Manager role, beating some tough competition to do so, in my last job as an 'employee'. At last, I was on my way! But as the harsh reality of the new role sank in and the inner work I was doing as part of my professional coaching qualifications created the necessary clarity around what I really wanted, I realised I was on the wrong path. That was quite a difficult time for me as I entered into the 'neutral zone' of my transition, trying to work out and feel a path forwards.

While in general there is no 'right' or a 'wrong' time to change direction, there are some exceptions. Making any drastic decisions to **act** within a year (certainly within 6 months) after a close bereavement is generally considered, in the long term, not to be helpful. Grief needs time to be worked through. The pain of loss may make some people reach out to affect change in aspects of their life that they do have control over, so move carefully here. As the saying goes; 'Act in haste, repent at your leisure'. 'The Grief Cycle' developed by Elizabeth Kubler-Ross explores how we all move through distinctive stages in our grieving process which might be helpful to take a look at if this situation applies to you. 'Step 2: Let Go' in this guide will help you make good any 'endings' that haven't yet been concluded for you.

Every individual should be best placed to be the judge of their own timing – but sometimes we need help getting the clarity around our situation, how we might be holding ourselves back, sabotaging our own efforts to move forward. There is a balance to be struck between moving too soon and leaving it too late – and we can get this wrong if we're not coming from a place of sincere self-awareness and understanding.

Get Out Of Your Comfort Zone

People can stay too long in a role, tolerating and 'making do' for many reasons. One is that we do tend to *like* to stay where it's comfortable, because it's just that, comfortable! Being human, we can't help but create '**comfort zones**' around ourselves. We establish routines, habits of behaviour and thought. We know what is expected of ourselves and can anticipate the likely outcomes from our relationships. Being in our comfort zone, things feel certain and familiar. In our work, things feel predictable, controllable and we generally feel competent. There is perhaps a sense of belonging and there is no threat to our identify or self-esteem.

Unfortunately we don't do so well, long term, if we stay within our comfort zone. We start to slow down and stop learning and growing. We can get stuck in our ways of thinking; things get stale and entrenched. To progress we need to move out of our comfort zone and into our **'stretch zone'**. This is where we are challenged; we are able to learn and change our thoughts, behaviours and habits. It feels a little edgy, a bit 'seat of the pants' and it can get uncomfortable. What is now demanded from us is to rise to the challenge and expand, whether that be in technical knowledge or emotional intelligence for example. Importantly, we must also have the self-belief and mind-set *to believe we can succeed*. That self-belief may have needed some effort and support to be activated, but it is there. If the shift is too great however, we shoot past this stretch and fall into **'panic' zone'** – which feels very different. (See diagram 1 below).

Diagram 1: Comfort, Stretch and Panic Zones

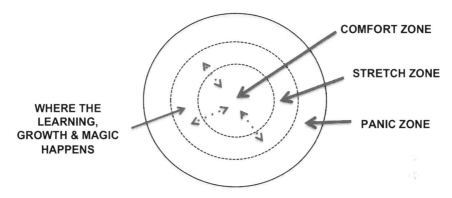

Avoid Panic, Work From Stretch

When we overshoot and end up in our panic zone, we feel stress, worry and fear. Some people get angry and feel hopeless or sad. There may be feelings of shame and guilt, frustration and inadequacy. When in this zone, the amygdala, that part of the brain that is scanning for threat or reward, is triggered to respond to what is going on as a threat. The neurophysiological response floods our body with cortisol, oxygen is diverted away from the brain and our pulse rate increases. We are preparing our body's large muscles for one of the threat responses - flight, fight, freeze or fold.

Unfortunately, our cognitive processing abilities substantially decrease in this state. In evolutionary terms when faced with a sabre-tooth tiger, it wasn't helpful to start thinking 'Ooh, a sabre-toothed tiger. Now I wonder it that's a male or a female. Is it hungry? Should I run?' Fortunately for the survival of our species, our reactions to such threats are part of our reptile or early brain that runs automatically. Our amygdala kicks in and our bodies respond accordingly.

When we are responding to a perceived threat, we lose our ability to think clearly, to process information, to relate to other people. We literally experience 'tunnel vision' as our peripheral vision function is affected. If you've ever experienced a situation where you've been challenged by a superior in work and you can't seem to find the right words, forget key facts and end up fumbling your way through – that's you feeling the effects of this 'amygdala hijack' on your cognitive processing.

One of the key factors determining whether we end up in our stretch zone or panic zone when it comes to thinking and acting on a desire for a career move is the **belief** that we can do it. Without that belief, we move into panic and we won't progress. As described above, when the cortisol stress response is running the show, we're not going to be able to think and act clearly. Managing our stress through being very mindful of our *mind-set* here is vital, which is why the 'Choose to Flourish' approach described in a later chapter focuses considerable attention on building and nurturing an empowering mind-set.

Another key factor is ensuring there is a sufficient feeling of *security and safety* involved in the change. I've found through working with my clients that without helping them to feel safe, they won't be able to leave their comfort zone and will remain stuck. Without support, they will often try to go about their career change in such a way that hurls them into the panic zone, where their fear and anxiety will freeze their energy and motivation and their efforts will all be in vain.

The Choose to Flourish approach is specially designed to ensure you are both *challenged* and *supported* so you work through the desired external change, and internal transition, in a way that moves you out of your comfort zone, and into your stretch zone, avoiding any slip into panic.

The **timing** of any career move can also affect the likelihood of avoiding the panic zone. These are some of the key points that should be considered.

➢ Start designing your move before external circumstances force you to take action from a place of panic rather than stretch

➢ Be mindful that the natural attractiveness of the comfort zone (and perhaps any attachment or need you place on security) may try to hold you back from seeking change

➢ Most people experience a certain about of fear about things being different. What successful people realise is that it's not lucky circumstances or being special in any way that has aided them making fortuitous career moves, it's their ability to manage that fear, create a tolerance around taking risk and so move forwards.

Courage is the first of human virtues because it makes all others possible

Aristotle

Before we leap into the ten steps for successful transitions taken from the 'Choose2Flourish' programme, it feels appropriate that I should share with you a little about my own story so you understand how I feel qualified to write this guide on how to change career and thrive in life.

> **Checklist for successful start to a career change**
>
> - ➢ Understand where you are in terms of internal transition.
> - ➢ Actively work on enhancing internal locus of control so you believe you are in charge of taking yourself forwards. Accept personal leadership.
> - ➢ Be aware of where you are in the novelty-mastery 7 year cycle.
> - ➢ Seek support.
> - ➢ Put yourself into a place of 'stretch' rather than 'panic' in your efforts to move out of any comfort zones.
> - ➢ Identify both the empowering beliefs and critical thought patterns going on inside your head. Nurture a supportive mind-set.
> - ➢ Listen to your heart; hear what your feelings are telling you.
> - ➢ Trust the universe is friendly
> - ➢ Be courageous.

CHAPTER 2

My Story

"All you need is courage Rhian, courage. Then everything will be okay"
My late Grandma, Hannah 'Nance' Pryce

I'm Rhian Sherrington: I'm an Executive and Confident Transitions Coach, author and speaker. I am passionate about enabling people to thrive in careers that feed their soul, as well as their bank balance. I specifically love guiding people through their transition into a more meaningful life, and a purpose-led career.

One of the reasons I have specialised as a confident transitions coach is that this is very much part of my own story. I have learnt over time, and sometimes the hard way, that there are vital steps to follow in order to successfully transition from one stage to the next.

For many people looking in at my life, I would appear fairly successful. I've been very fortunate in that for the most part, I've been able to find the courage to follow my heart. The words of my late Grandma were tremendously influential, and I've tried to lead my life by them. There was a time, however, when I forgot to do so, at considerable pain to myself. In truth it took until I turned 40 to fully realise a vital aspect to living a 'courageous life' that I'll come to in a moment.

That ability to follow my heart has led to some very interesting career choices. I remember being challenged by my peers at Oxford University as to why I wasn't going after the big corporate jobs they were seeking. I knew, however, that wasn't for me. My values were focused

— 17 —

around wanting to make a difference for the planet, and I was able, for a long while, to believe I was doing that in the best way I could.

I set up and ran a small youth expeditions company for a while, travelling with groups to Ecuador. I worked as a geography field studies teacher, in the wilds of Scotland as well as in more accessible Devon. I had a stint as an adviser for the UK government, and I worked for big a UK charity. For the most part, all these roles, these career changes, allowed me to follow my truth, my values. I was moving on up in the organisations I worked in and outwardly as I said, it made me look very successful.

Inside, however, was another story. I was hiding a deep truth, which only become clear to me much later. I really lacked confidence. I was actually quite scared of people, and I would often hold myself aloof in order to protect myself from emotional hurt. Whilst I may have shown tremendous physical courage (scaling glaciers, exploring hidden valleys and passes during a university expedition to Northern Pakistan for example), I was at the same time unable to sum up the emotional courage to be truly myself with other people. At the same time, I would also be seeking validation. I needed external validation in order to create a sense of my own worth. This manifested itself in all sorts of relationship agonies and disasters, as well as underselling my career ambitions and myself. So on one hand, I was following my heart, being courageous and on the other, I was hiding from my potential and my real self.

I muddled through, met and married a wonderful man. (This remains something I'm rather amazed by. Having been bridesmaid to four close friends and entering my thirties clearly single, I was starting to believe there wasn't anyone special out there for me. Reaching our 10th Wedding Anniversary this year, I'm glad I was wrong there).

It wasn't until we had our children that my working life started to get difficult and my ability to be courageous and follow my heart wobbled.

Perhaps that resonates with some of you reading this right now. Because I was unable to make my choices based solely on what my heart wanted, I had to push things to one side. We moved and I changed jobs because of my husband's career, and after I had my son, I was juggling part-time work with being a mum. Whilst that was, and remains, incredibly rewarding, I was getting very exhausted and without really being fully conscious of it. I was tolerating a lot of stuff that was wearing me down. When on maternity leave with my daughter, I remember telling my mother in law that I was going to go and do something different. But a year later, there I was back in the same organization, and desperately unhappy with the internal politics, the difficult people. I had started my professional coaching qualifications at that point and things were starting to shift, but I thought I could still keep building a successful career inside that organization.

In hindsight, my need for security was a strong motivating factor for me. Combined with the insidious wearing down of my confidence that comes from not feeling valued, I was unable to stop and really listen to myself. So outwardly things would have looked fine, that I was doing really well. My family were fantastic, I had a great husband, thriving children, a beautiful home and a good career. Inwardly though that just wasn't the case and my health started to reflect the stress and incongruence I was experiencing. I had a painful eye condition that wouldn't go away and put on quite a lot of weight.

I find it hard to look back at this time now because I don't really recognize the person I was. Weeping on the sofa after work became fairly normal, and I felt very powerless to change anything. Whilst I didn't fall back into the 'why me?' trap I'd been in when I was younger, I couldn't see a way out of where I was. I'd been promoted and should have been incredibly happy at the senior position I was now in. But I wasn't. I was desperately unhappy and very stressed. But then it happened; the bolt from the blue and whilst I'd change in an instant what happened if I could, a turning point came in my life and everything changed forever.

My wonderful brother in law took his own life. It was absolutely devastating. If you're reading this and have experienced that sort of sudden bereavement, I really reach out to you. It shakes your world completely. But what I've since learnt was there was a gift in that tragedy. And whilst it's taken time and more heartbreak to work through the fall out, and feelings of guilt, that loss did become a real turning point. Because as I saw that devastation in my loved ones and made myself look fully at the sadness of what had happened, I realised I had stopped following my heart. I had stopping living my life with courage. I was letting me fears and insecurities determine what I could or couldn't do. I now realised I had to live my life to the full.

I had to overcome my fear, my lack of confidence, my fear of people, all the messy stuff that was holding me back. I had to now pursue my talent, my strengths. I knew I wanted to help others transform and transition into meaningful and purpose led careers, especially where those people wanted to make a positive difference to our planet. I've since been on even more of a journey as I've evolved into running a business rather than being an employee. I've had to re-learn my rules, evaluate my values and set boundaries in order to effectively juggle my work around my children. The external change of running a business has required a substantial inner transition into becoming a businesswoman.

Nurturing a positive and powerful inner world, my mind-set, has perhaps been the hardest aspect of this personal transition. Seeking external support has been vital in this regard, and I'm very grateful to the various coaches, guides and programmes I have sought out and worked with. There is a real temptation in our society to believe we can 'work it out' all on our own. That is clearly not the case. The sooner we recognise and get comfortable with inter-dependence rather than seeking an exhausting and unsustainable state of independence the better – for us as individuals, as well as for our communities and society.

Now I'm fully able to 'choose to flourish' and I'm grateful for every single opportunity I have had to do that. I don't believe you need trauma in your life to make a significant career change, but we often do need something, some kind of trigger to make us realise that the status quo is untenable.

There's a model called 'The Change Equation' that is often referred to in organisational change management. Developed by Beckhard and Harris (1987) based on previously work done by Gleicher, it states that for the practical first steps in change to occur (C), the attractive vision (A) and the discomfort with the present (B) must be *greater than* the pain involved in changing, the 'resistance' (D).

Change Equation

Gleicher, Beckhard, Harris

$$C = A + B + C > D$$

C = Desired change

A = Attractive vision

B = Discomfort with the present

C = Practical first steps towards the vision

D = Pain involved in changing

For all of the participants on my Mastermind Programme or clients working with me privately, this formula simplifies an essential truth.

- ➤ Nothing will change in your working life if you are unable to find an inspiring vision of your future.

- ➤ If you fail to identify the pain and discomfort with where you are right now, it is highly unlikely you will overcome the inertia and friction stemming from the pain involved in changing.

> Even with a vision and awareness of the discomfort of the present, if you cannot find or commit to actions that give you the practical first steps, you will not be successful in moving on.

We'll come back to this model later, but for now, I hope I've given you sufficient insight into why I do what I do. My clients tell me that through working with me they've been able to access a level of freedom, clarity, self-belief and confidence they never thought possible. I hope you'll be able to develop the same.

You may have picked up through reading my story and the previous chapter that I don't believe purely seeking financial reward is the way to a thriving and successful career. A happy and satisfying career is one where our values and needs are being met, in an environment that both supports and challenges us. Whilst financial reward is certainly important, the degree of importance it has for each individual will vary. But for **all of us,** we are not going to ultimately thrive if we're fulfilling someone else's ambitions for us. We will flounder if we're applying a measure of success that has no intrinsic value for us. Understanding what it truly means to flourish will empower us to recognise what we need in our lives, in our work, thus supporting a successful transition into a new career.

CHAPTER 3

What is 'Flourishing'?

'Choosing to flourish' for many people means becoming empowered to be themselves. Accepting personal responsibility for the choices we're making in our lives is a vital part of the process. Importantly, when we start to recognise those choices we are making *unconsciously*, we can begin to overcome what is preventing us from really living the life we truly want and enjoying the career we desire to have. Hence choosing to flourish often involves a re-think of our career direction.

I believe we can all thrive when we:

1. Find the courage to really follow our hearts; and

2. Align our strengths and our passion to really making a difference to the world, whether that be in your neighbourhood or on a global scale.

In naming my business and coaching programmes 'Choose2Flourish' I wanted to highlight the conscious effort required in designing a life that enables us to be happy and fulfilled.

'She's flourishing. He's just flourishing'. Don't you hope someone can say that about you? It conjures up a smiling face, a relaxed demeanour, someone directing their lives, master (or mistress) of who they are and where they're going. It feels a fun place to be; the positivity and happiness is easy to grasp, as is perhaps a sense of purpose, of fulfilment. Surely that's the best goal to have for a productive life?

The Oxford University Dictionary defines 'flourish' (vb) as *'a living organism that grows in a healthy or vigorous way, especially as the result of a particularly congenial environment'.* That 'congenial environment' for humans is now increasingly understood as one that nurtures our whole 'well-being' and is something that we can consciously create and cultivate in our lives, families, organisations and wider society. It's what we need to thrive.

Well being matters because we live healthier, longer, more rounded, more productive, creative, satisfied lives when we are thriving compared to when we are not. When a parent is asked what they most want for their children, all the answers (e.g. happiness, love, joy, success, doing what they love to do, having meaning in their lives, health etc.) all boil down to the same thing – well being.

According to Dr Martin Seligman, a world-renowned positive psychologist:

"It is all too commonplace not be mentally ill but to be stuck and languishing in life. Positive mental health is a presence; the presence of positive health; the presence of engagement, the presence of meaning, the presence of good relationships and the presence of accomplishment. Being in a state of mental health is not merely disorder free; rather it is the presence of flourishing".

'Flourish' is a word that has been growing in importance and resonance across western society. When I first chose 'Choose2Flourish Ltd' for my company name in 2011 many people challenged me on the relevance of the word 'flourish'. They felt it wasn't in the public's consciousness enough for it to work as a memorable business name. I trusted my intuition, my gut feeling, and held fast. And I'm glad that I did.

Flourishing provides an inspiring challenge to singular, wealth based definitions for our happiness, and provides a measurable goal for our lives, organisations and communities. Martin Seligman defined 'flourishing' in his book "Flourish' (2011) as being the end goal for 'well being'. He defines 'flourishing' as a construct made up of 5 elements or 'pillars' that can be measured, objectively as well as subjectively. These 5 elements (PERMA) are:

- **Positive emotions** – such as feelings of joy, achievement, pride, love, gratitude; having life satisfaction and happiness,

- **Engagement** – for example being 'in flow' at work, losing all track of time doing something that engages you completely,

- **Positive Relationships** – such as being connected to other people, undertaking acts of kindness for others,

- **Meaning** – believing in something bigger than ourselves,

- **Accomplishment** – having mastery over ourselves, achieving and progressing in those things most important to us.

For most people, our work is a dominant feature of our waking hours. It is therefore vital we look at these 5 elements or pillars and see how they can be experienced in work, in our careers.

Felicity Huppert and Timothy So, from the University of Cambridge's Well Being Institute, surveyed a representative 43,000 adults from 23 European countries. The results of this work defined a 'flourishing individual' as having all the 'core' features listed below, and 3 out of 6 'additional features. Based on this definition, Denmark tops the charts with 33 per cent of its population deemed to be flourishing and the UK languishing behind with only 18 per cent identified as flourishing.

Core features:

- Positive emotion

- Engagement, interest

- Meaning, purpose

Additional features:

- Self-esteem

- Optimism

- Resilience

- Vitality

- Self-determination

- Positive relationships

The Choose2Flourish Programme is built on the premise that whilst we may all have different drivers influencing our career choices (such as our values and lived experiences), when we are able to experience these 5 pillars to flourishing through our work, our careers take on the fullest value and meaning. Whilst of course there is far more to life than just work, when we do find a path that enables us to flourish in, and through, our work, it positively impacts on many other aspects of our life.

The Power of the Positive

Numerous studies highlight the importance of positivity and positive relationships on our well-being. Therefore, being aware of our emotions, of what is influencing and controlling our feelings, is very beneficial. One aspect of self that is developed through the Choose2Flourish approach is learning to tap into and trust our feelings as a guide to what is really going on in our lives.

How aware are you of your feelings? Do you know exactly what is going on when you are joyful or get angry?

Emotions give us signals as to whether or not we are on course. They bring our attention to something we need to take notice of. Emotions start with a **thought,** they generate a **feeling**, which then motivates us to **act.** By being aware of the thought that generated the feeling, we can **choose** how we then respond. There is, or at least there can be, a gap between a stimulus and our response - and it is in this gap that we can make a conscious decision as to how we are going to act. This requires us to be highly self-aware and then to develop ways in which we can build our mental capacity for self-mastery – all key parts of enabling us to be more positive.

Our genetic make-up determines about 50% of our tendency towards 'half full or half empty' optimistic or pessimistic world-views. That still leaves a lot we can do to build more positive emotion into our daily lives, including gratitude, serenity, interest, hope, pride, amusement, inspiration, awe, joy and love.

This matters, as research suggests that positive emotion is tremendously important to our well-being, impacting on our health, our resilience and our performance. In her book 'Positivity' Dr Barbara Fredrickson (2009) provides an easy to read synopsis of the science and resulting advice. The headlines from her findings on positivity were:

It makes us feel good – the more you cultivate it, the more you have; the more you have, the more you can draw upon it and use your own awareness of its impacts to help others build it into their lives. Human beings are *naturally wired to see the negative.* We have to <u>proactively</u> seek out the 'good stuff' to help us balance out that hard wiring.

Health – decades of research has proven that excess stress kills people. We now also know that heart-felt, positive emotion (i.e. real, not faked!), is good for us. Optimists live longer, with a lower risk of stroke and heart disease.

Resilience – positive emotion helps people bounce back quickly from setbacks and helps to steer a steady course through challenge and change.

Performance – positivity keeps our brains open, making us more receptive to new ideas, to learning, helping us be creative and have empathy for others. All of that combines to improve productivity at work, at school, helping us move forward with our life goals and aspirations.

Having an awareness of the above is important. It can counter some of the arguments, excuses and limiting beliefs offered by people who don't understand the power of these principles to flourishing and who might wish to question your need for a career change, based on a desire to find more meaning, purpose or enjoyment. Statements might include;

> ➢ You can't and shouldn't expect work to make you happy;

> ➢ Happiness doesn't matter – earning money is all that counts;

> ➢ Feeling good about your work is a luxury for the few – you can't expect to *enjoy* your job;

> ➢ Hard work brings success – if it doesn't feel like hard work, you're not doing it right.

> ➢ Any job is better than none.

> ➢ You should be grateful for what you've got.

I like to challenge those attitudes and encourage you to do the same. If being happy in your work has such a beneficial impact on your performance, imagine what solutions could be created for the problems facing today's world if those working on them were able to thrive in those roles? What would society look like if we were all encouraged to find out what really lights us up and were then able to apply our strengths to issues, situations and people we cared about? What if identifying our strengths, values and discovering what was really important to us was an integral part of our education system?

Reflecting on what you need to have in your working life is empowering. Moving away from defining yourself by a job title or salary scale allows you to be open to the fullest possibility of 'you'. Feeling engaged, able to find meaning and purpose in your work is a vital aspect to enjoying a thriving career and we move into exploring that next.

Engagement, Meaning and Accomplishment in Work

Based on research into what makes for a fulfilling life, Martin Seligman describes three pathways. These are:

> - **The Pleasurable Life** – where we pursue things that are purely for fun, for pleasure.

> - **The Engaged Life** – were we pursue things that really absorb our attention and interest; and

> - **The Meaningful Life** – where we do things to contribute to something bigger than ourselves.

The approach that leaves us feeling far happier and satisfied for longer is the one that combines doing things for others in pursuit of something meaningful to us – **a combination of the engaged and meaningful life.** If you can also incorporate aspect that are pleasurable to you in the pursuit of this, than even better!

In our hearts, I think most of us want to do meaningful work that we're engaged with, and from which we gain satisfaction and a sense of accomplishment. Difficulties arise if we have never found out what kind of work that would be. Sometimes we set out on our careers knowing, but for a multitude of reasons, lose that understanding about ourselves along the way. We can 'fall into' a career path without thinking too deeply about our long-term satisfaction or how that is creating meaning for us.

When I started out on my working life, a guiding principle was around whether or not it was going to be fun as well as interesting. I enjoyed working outdoors and with young people. Teaching geography field studies I was able to share my love of the Scottish wilderness whilst inspiring them (I hope) to think for themselves and appreciate the story of the landscape unfolding in front of them. However after a year I knew I had reached a dead end. The novelty of learning what to do was over. Whilst I still felt it was meaningful work, I was faced with a level of repetition that wasn't going to maintain my engagement. Whilst I was able to extend my teaching for another 5 years through moving to a different part of the UK, ultimately I knew I would have to change direction.

Seeking more meaning and purpose is part of the natural cycle of ageing that we need to recognise as of the many transition phases of life. Resisting it by telling ourselves we're too old to change now, that we're being 'silly' and will 'snap out of it' pushes the process further inside us, where it festers but won't disappear. Disappointment makes us very critical. I'm sure you know people who have become sour. Don't let that happen to you because you didn't listen to your call to seek out meaningful and engaging work.

The Money Question

"Money alone cannot win success. Money is a reward for playing the game well. It is not the game."
Robert Holder, PhD

Material reward does not guarantee a flourishing career. A career direction that fulfils a purpose, meets a need, solves a problem or in some way 'serves' can be a more significant factor. I know there is nothing new in that statement, but there are still many people who make significant job decisions based primarily on whether or not it represents a pay rise. Of course, material reward is important – it brings with it the possibility of a certain quality of life and our happiness is linked to an extent to income. Do bear in mind, however, that the research suggests that there is a **limit** to this. Once certain needs are met, our happiness and wellbeing does not increase as we earn more money. Interestingly some studies also suggest that *how* and *where* we spend our money strongly determines our levels of satisfaction from having it. If we are able to make our money work for the 'greater good' then that can be a very inspiring and motivating place to operate from. Tapping into that as part of your personal vision (see Step 6) might also help you avoid a common money trap that some unconsciously fall into. That is, believing financial reward and 'doing good' are polar opposites and hence, you cannot have both.

Many people who are 'values led' in their career choices, who want to make a difference to the world, fall into this trap of equating financial reward to somehow being 'bad'. This is not helped by the fact that some work, such as in the environmental, charity and health care sectors, where you'd expect to find tremendous meaning, can be low paid. While there is a wider societal question of how some roles are arguably 'undervalued', lets stay focused on the individual level here. There are many limiting beliefs people can hold around making money and understanding our relationship to it is an important part of raising awareness of our career choices and drivers.

How much money is enough? Often we are unclear as we have no idea how much we *spend* and how much we actually *need*. Without going into too much detail, it's important we work out our incomings and outgoings and understand our financial situation. So many clients who start my programmes have very little awareness of their current financial situation. Many are deeply uncomfortable approaching it due to all the negative baggage they have around money. Like any unhelpful beliefs, we can re-wire these to be far more empowering, leading to more supportive and aligned behaviour.

For now, lets consider developing an awareness for just 3 figures. That is;

> Our lowest figure of income that will cover the essential basics – rent or mortgage, bills, food, taxes, etc.

> Our middle figure, the income level that covers the basics whilst also providing for some savings, contributing to a pension, a holiday etc. Finally, we should have in our minds (and written down);

> Our top figure, our 'wildest dreams' figure of income, monthly or yearly. This of course will vary hugely from individual to individual. Don't be led by what you think you *should* earn. Be led by what you think is right for you, being open to new possibilities but also listening to your heart and your values.

Once you have these figures in mind, you are in a far better place to set some financial parameters around your job search, or new business goals. When lots of things feel uncertain and up in the air, having a few figures to hand can be very grounding. It can certainly provide hard evidence of how much you actually need to earn in the first instance. It can be amazing how such clarity can trigger tremendous resourcefulness and creativity when combined with the motivation to move on. Remember: It's a combination of meaning, accomplishment and purpose that are the cornerstones to a fulfilling career. Financial rewards have their limits in creating happiness but you need your levels of expectation to be clear.

Finding Our Meaning and Purpose

For some, having a purpose in life can feel uncomfortable. If you're an atheist or agnostic, the suggestion of having to have *purpose*, which is sometimes seen as something divinely driven, is not going to be helpful. For others, seeing themselves as part of an inter-connected conscious universe flowing from an underlying spiritual or God entity can be incredible strengthening and uplifting. Setting aside any connotation to a belief system, understanding the 'why' behind what you do or want to do, can make all the difference to whether you follow through or give up at the first hurdle. Asking **'Why am I doing this? Why do I want to do this? What purpose does this serve and who for?** is a vital part of working through 'Step 6' in Chapter 5.

When you've got purpose, you find focus. Some people have so many different ideas about what they could be doing that they end up doing nothing different at all - because they didn't know which one to follow. Identifying your purpose is *"a filter to making important decisions"* according to Within People, an international organisation that helps business leaders connect to their purpose. Purpose is not a goal – we don't have targets. Purpose is what helps us find the right opportunities and make authentic choices.

"A vision is a rich picture of our imagined future. Our purpose guides us towards that dream. But it isn't a strategy or a plan – it's the passion that keeps us motivated"

Within People

Linked to this is the importance of recognising that purpose can't be found by changing something in your *external* condition. There is a temptation when things get difficult to move on, to find a new relationship, job or place to live. Without knowing what it is you are seeking, it is highly unlikely these external changes will satisfy you for long. Looking inside ourselves can be painful but purpose, however, is something you have to find **inside**. If you need to come to terms with anything traumatic in your background, seeking professional help is essential. If you're flip-flopping between ideas, then you've not finished reflecting and doing the 'inner work' required to achieve a successful transition to a new direction. You may well still be in the 'neutral zone' of transition. Purpose is found through investigating your desires and we explore this in more detail in Chapter 5.

— 33 —

Recognising Accomplishment

Whilst experiencing accomplishment in our work is a vital aspect of flourishing, we can, unfortunately, get in our own way of feeling this sense of achievement. Owning our abilities is a necessary skill but because of our hard wiring towards negativity we can often forget to see our accomplishments for what they are. Where this can show up to our detriment is discounting our abilities when comparing ourselves to others, especially if we are looking at them to see if we could do what they are doing. For example, viewing the profiles of people already working at the company you wish to join. Whilst seeking out information about others in this way is a good strategy for examining future alternatives, negative comparison and downgrading our own abilities is not.

Fortunately, even the most self-effacing individual can learn to notice and recognise their accomplishments, with practice. Tools we use to great effect within the Choose2Flourish programme are seeking feedback from others and keeping a log of what we've done well – such as a 'Brilliant me' folder. This is not some sort of egotistical activity but a vital exercise in supporting an empowering mind-set (see step 8 in the process described in Chapter 5).

Positive Relationships

Relationships are an essential part of our satisfaction and happiness in life. John Donne clearly recognised this in his poem, 'Devotions' where he states 'No man is an island'. We are social beings who need others to thrive. If we are to flourish, we need to take the time and energy to consider the quality of our relationships in all aspects of our life.

Given that we spend so much time in work, enjoying positive relationships with our colleagues is a significant aspect to thriving in our career.

Going back to the earlier point about understanding your purpose, we also need to have this inner understanding of who we are in work, and how we relate and communicate with others in order to be clear around our reasons for wanting to move away. Sometimes we may be *reacting* to the 'push' of things going wrong in our relationships rather than the 'pull' of us seeking out new challenges, meaning and purpose. Step 1 in the process described in Chapter 5 encourages you to reflect on what is *really* going on as sometimes staying put and focusing on improving the relationships (as well as your job role and responsibilities) may be what is required, rather than seeking to leap elsewhere.

The very first relationship we need to consider here though is with our self. Three questions that are helpful to reflect on are;

> **How truly do you like yourself?**

> **How authentic are you at work?**

> **How satisfied are you that your 'inner voice' (we all have one) supports you?** On a scale of 1 to 10, where 10 is a rock solid, positive, empowering voice and 1 is a deeply critical, totally unhelpful internal critic that poisons your self worth and self-belief.

> **Where do you score yourself?** (Can I just point out, very low scores here, combined with a low mood, could suggest you need the support of a medical professional. Don't suffer on your own – seek help).

Starting with that last question first: many people have an inner critic that can pop up to destabilise us at the most unhelpful times. This voice (described so well as a 'thought monkey' by one of my clients) can take on many guises, which, if left unchallenged, can really sabotage our intentions and desires. Working with a skilled coach is one powerful means of taming this critic and switching things around so that you can proactively retune this voice to support and empower, not squash and belittle, you. People who have gone through the Choose2Flourish Programme have really valued the way in which they've been able to rebuild their 'inner monkeys' into far more amenable and helpful creatures. We explore this in Step 8 of the process described in Chapter 5.

We should also consider whether we are 'playing' at being someone else at work. A lot has been written about the pros and cons of being our 'authentic' selves. Brené Brown's TED talk "The Power of Vulnerability' went viral when it first came out in 2010 and her book 'Daring Greatly' (2009) offers a powerful argument for allowing ourselves to be authentic as well as suggesting some helpful enabling tools. Simply reflecting on how authentic we're being can offer insight when it comes to considering a career change. When we are able to be ourselves, we can fully bring our strengths and passion into what we are doing. Hiding or pretending to be someone we're not depletes our energy and reduces our levels of satisfaction as we're probably not being able to accomplish things in the way we want. You may not feel able to be yourself because you are inhibited by your status or role. Rectifying this may change how you feel about your work and remove the perceived need to move. However if the inability to be authentic is due to the work place culture, then moving on may be the better option.

Whilst being authentic and liking yourself is key, enjoying positive relationships with colleagues is also very important. Accordingly you need to view your relationships with others as something you should never stop improving. We can all be better listeners, better communicators, and going back to Stephen R. Covey (2004) in '7 Habits of Highly Successful People', he couldn't have put it more succinctly when he identified Habit 5 as '**seek first to understand then to be understood**'. What a fine piece of advice to take into building positive relationships.

Check List for 'Flourishing' in Work

➤ Seligman's 'PERMA, 5 Pillars to Flourishing' model is a useful starting point to reflect on what you need to feel satisfied, purposeful, happy and productive.

➤ Getting clear on what *you* need to flourish is essential groundwork for a successful and thriving career.

➤ We all need meaning and purpose – it provides the filter through which we can judge all our decisions and opportunities.

➤ The ability to be ourselves, like ourselves and successfully connect with others forms a hidden backbone to our working lives that we shouldn't forget.

➤ Sometimes staying put is the best career change we need to make.

CHAPTER 4

The Choose to Flourish Approach

You have brains in your head
You have feet in your shoes
You can steer yourself any
Direction you choose

attributed to Dr Seuss

The solution I offer with my Choose2Flourish programme comes from a melting pot of learned experience – both my clients and my own. The key in this process is helping people:

➤ Find their **courage** so that they can **listen to their hearts**;

➤ Tune into their **intuition**; and

➤ Build their **confidence** to become the person that they're meant to be.

When you create an internal landscape that tolerates the unknown, can see possibilities and can trust, the ability to bring about longed for career shifts will come about. I won't lie and say this is an easy process if you need to work on some, or all, of the three aspects above. Some people who have a rare combination of high internal locus of control, a behavioural preference geared to direct action and a considerable amount of support behind the scenes, may appear to make their career changes with considerable ease. However, it's unlikely people of that ilk, who really are few and far between, will be reading this book!

— 39 —

Fundamental to my approach is pulling together research from the fields of positive psychology and neuroscience alongside the more spiritual, personal transformation literature. The ten-step guide outlined here offers a real blending of mind, body and spirit to empower and support people successfully through their career transitions. I've used this approach on myself transitioning from being an unhappy employee to being an author, professional coach, trainer and businesswoman, following my values and working with the people I want to be supporting. An avid life-long learner with twenty-five plus years of studying personal development, leadership as well as spiritual writings, I've combined my professional experience of organisational change management and creating sustained behaviour change with a holistic approach to working with people going through change, especially those seeking transformation in their careers.

The changes and shifts that come from these ten steps are profound. Every individual has their own set of issues that they need to work through in their own transition. The rate at which people move depends on where they are in their transformation journey. I've found that clients experience real key insights within the first month or two, and then start to work on embedding those shifts. At the end of six months, major changes have happened and the internal transition has been understood, supported and skilfully navigated. Participants are then well on their way to creating that career and that lifestyle they've been yearning for.

Every person's journey is different, and importantly new, more positive habits take time to be embedded. As I discuss in the paragraph below, our brains are plastic. Neuroscience is showing that we can rewrite our neural pathways, and actually create new ways of thinking. We can turn our new ways of thinking into new supportive behaviours and empowering beliefs. With effort, we can strengthen a weak internal 'locus of control'. To really embed new thoughts and turn them into new behaviours and habits does however, take a little bit of time and persistence. Anywhere from a month, to perhaps 6 months, or a year. That's how quickly people can expect to work through their transformation and really change their path.

Case Study: From Employee to Successful Businesswomen

Sarah came to me because she was setting herself up in her own business. She thought she was ready for doing this, but things were not panning out how she had imagined. She was unable to set goals or even create a vision for the business. This was really affecting her ability to attract new clients. She was very anxious and her energy levels were very low. Everything was coming from a highly stressed and distressed state.

Sarah expected to move into this new career path instantly - a very common expectation if you don't understand changes and transition. She wanted to move on to her new beginning really quickly. But the transition isn't like that – it's got three distinct stages, which if you fail to manage effectively, are likely to sabotage you and keep you stuck.

With Sarah we first of all had to bring things to their 'ending'. There were a lot of issues she needed to let go of, and we did that first. That created a new depth of understanding about herself and allowed space for new thoughts to rise up to her consciousness to be explored and understood. After that we worked to define and clarify what she needed to do and she was then able to start to find her vision, to identify her purpose. The programme then enabled her to move confidently into her new beginning, transforming from an insecure, frustrated and overtly anxious person, to a vibrant, dynamic woman, with a thriving business and flourishing perspective on life.

Change Your Mind

For more than 400 years, the brain was considered to be something of a machine, with different parts to do specific jobs, which deteriorated over time until all its functions eventually ceased. This has now been categorically disproven. Whilst dead cells can't be repaired, the brain can grow new cells and continue to develop – 'use it or lose it' being a common refrain. Developments in scanning technology, such as MRI and fMRI scans that allow us to see brain structure and brain activity respectively, have enabled us to understand, like never before, what is going on inside the living brain.

The building blocks inside our brains are neurons. These brain cells either do 'a job' or hold the structure for the other neurons. Through a mixed pulse of electricity and chemical activity, neurons form connections. Firing off together, they 'wire together', creating pathways. Greater brain activity stimulates further activity, with a growth in new pathways between the neurons. Our understanding of the brain has now been radically changed by an appreciation of how 'plastic' the brain really is.

Neuroplasticity is the property of the brain to change. The brain can change in a number of ways (Brann, 2015). Traditionally, the early years of life and puberty, leading into the early 20's, have been seen as key years of brain growth and development. After that, it had been commonly assumed that we endure a slow but relentless process of gentle deterioration. The unexpected recovery of function in stroke and brain injury patients, has, however, led to a re-appraisal of this belief. Through this emerging science, we now know neurogenesis (the creation of new neurons) and cortical remapping (finding new pathways between neurons) can occur throughout life. Behaviour changes, environmental changes and thoughts can all effect change in neural pathways (Brann 2015). We can develop new ways of thinking and behaving, meaning that we can change our neural pathways and learn different behaviours, different habits.

In my previous book, '**Alchemy for the Mind: Create Your Confident Core**' (available on Amazon, Nook and Kobo platforms), I explored in more detail how the brain works and the role the mind has in creating the new neural pathways that leads to new behaviour and new habits. The important thing to note here is this: If you believe you are the creator of your thoughts, you have the power to change them. By thinking new thoughts about yourself, choosing alternative courses of action, you can alter how you behave and the habits you may have fallen into.

In approaching a career change, it is vital that you cultivate a belief and a mind-set that you can do it, that you will succeed. If you need to build your confidence and self-belief around that then remember; confidence is a skill, a thought pattern you can learn and a feeling you can generate inside. Through the 10 Steps outlined in Chapter 5, we pay real attention to this essential process.

Find Your Courage

Aristotle said the highest of all human virtues was courage as it allowed all the rest. Having courage enables us to move through risk and uncertainty, or as Ernest Hemingway saw it '*having grace under pressure*'. Many personal development thought leaders, inspirational figureheads and authors have been quoted as saying how important courage is to us all in living a full and meaningful life. One of my personal favourites that resonates strongly with me is attributed to Nelson Mandela:

"Courage is not the absence of fear. It is inspiring others to move beyond it".

I also agree with Bev James, Executive Coach and CEO of The Coaching Academy when she said:

"Be Brave. The next level of success always lies slightly outside your current confidence zone"

Courage is what enables us to rise above what we fear, and stops fear from holding us back. Each one of us can do this but we all have our own personal scales as to how big or small the fear or challenge to be overcome is. In any career change, there is always a need to be courageous. You don't have a 100% guarantee that what you want to move into will work out exactly as you hope. In listening to your heart there are risks, and working through your needs, getting clarity on your dreams and taking action to realise the change requires you to face a whole number of things you may fear.

Courage might be a virtue, but it is also an experience, a skill and belief. Psychologists who treat people with life limiting phobias have shown how repeated exposure to what they fear actually lowers the body's psychological fear response. Neuroscientists believe they have now identified what they call the 'courage centre' in the brain (sgACC – the subgenual anterior cingulate cortex) and early studies suggest this can override the fear response controlled by the brain's amygdala. The amygdala stays quiet so your body stays in neutral and you don't have the rapid pulse, clammy, perspiring skin or loss of mental cognition.

Having that experience of practising being courageous builds up a memory bank of positive experiences that can be recalled, and drawn upon, when other new, fearful situations present themselves. Developing the skill of making ourselves more courageous is possible – it just needs practise and effort. We can choose to believe whether or not we have courage, just as we can choose to believe, or not, that we are confident. And the two are linked. Practising overcoming small things that make you fearful gives you the evidence you need to show that you are someone who can overcome a fear. At the heart of all confidence issues is a fear, such as a fear of failure or of not being good enough. When you can see that you are someone who can overcome fear, when the evidence for that is easily accessible to you, then having courage allows you to find the confidence to be who you really are, do the things you are meant to do and fulfil your life in its entirety.

— 44 —

This is neuroplasticity in action. New neural pathways are being created inside the brain as we learn to change our behaviour, through changing our beliefs and our thoughts. Through repetition, these new behaviours can become new habits. It is said to take up to 31 consecutive days for a new habit, for a new neural pathway to be created – any break and the count needs to start again from the beginning! (The Coaching Academy, 2012).

However, certain conditions need to be met for new cell growth (neurogenesis). We do need to be focused, stimulated and return regularly to that area of new learning, and do our reviewing and reflecting in a safe environment. It is exciting to see how advances in neuroscience are supporting what we 'know' about coaching. That is, coaching helps people successfully transform their inner and outer worlds to tremendous effect.

Ditch the Sat Nav

Many people start their working lives 'making do'. Especially in the challenging climate faced by today's graduates, having *any* job is often preferable to sitting in your parents' house wondering when your life will start. I understand that. My very first paid job, excluding the fast food joints, nightclubs and clothing retailers that provided some financial support whilst studying for my degrees, was working as a University Demonstrator and assistant. I never had any intention of staying in academia but it was a start. And, importantly, it was using some of my key strengths that, despite the lack of self-insight in my early twenties, I had already identified.

I'd realised I liked talking to groups, that I was good at inspiring others. I moved on to many different things from that launching point, improving my ability each time to listen to my heart, my values, to find my courage to make conscious decisions around each move. However, many people do not, and end up, 10, 20 years down the line, in a career that they made *no conscious decision* to get into in the first place. You probably know at least two people who've done just that – perhaps that's also you.

In such cases, it's like being plugged into a sat nav system that takes people through their lives on autopilot. In such a place, you're accepting directions not choosing them yourself. With the sat nav system switched on, you're not encouraged to think, to look deep inside yourself. There is no incentive to question and wonder at what is really going on. Where do I really want to go? Is this all there is to me? There are many reasons why this happens, such as a lack of self-belief and self-efficacy due past experiences and influences, such as beliefs and behaviours of parents or other significant adults during childhood.

Not being conscious of the choices we're making does not bode well for being able to truly flourish in life. It's likely that sooner or later, that sat nav system will fail and that person will find themselves lost. In my 'Choose2Flourish' approach I encourage my clients to unplug from that sat nav and find their own way. This means discovering their own individual map and navigating by their own internal compass, to really enjoy and 'own' their journey.

Your Flourishing Map and Compass

Life is a journey. It's an adventure and when you are exploring new horizons, it's best to have some means to navigate your way. In developing what I have called your 'Flourishing Compass', you are taken through a process that identifies four essential aspects of self-insight and understanding that are necessary for successfully transitioning into a new career or role. We go into more detail in Chapter 5, Steps 3 and 4 but to briefly summarise here, the points on the Flourishing Compass are:

> ➢ **North - What you do need?** This is about helping clients really understand what it is they truly need in their life. What's important to them.

- **East – What do you enjoy? How do you get into 'flow'?** We need an understanding of our passions, our interests. What gets us so focused we lose track of time? This point of the compass also stands for 'energy'. Being aware of what nurtures or depletes our energy levels provides a powerful means by which to navigating our choices.

- **South - What are your strengths? How are you using them?** South also stands for stories, because as human beings we're great at creating these stories of our lives inside our head. Sometimes they can be very powerful, but sometimes the script needs to be stopped. We need to recognize it for the limiting story line that it is, and we need to create a new story.

- **West – Where is your will?** Nothing will happen if we lack motivation. Desire is the vital powerhouse to overcoming the inertia of our 'comfort zones' and the discomfort of changing.

With the Choose2Flourish approach, we develop a supportive and enquiring *mind-se*t to seeing the change we are contemplating and the transition we are in as a journey. We remain open to not knowing all the answers at the start and for most people this involves building up their tolerance of change and taking a risk. In addition, as well as creating your internal navigation system through your 'flourishing compass', we build a map. Each individual needs to find his or her own unique map. In order to do this, answers to the following key framing questions need to be found;

- What's **the scale** of your map? – What kind of **time frame** are you comfortable with and energised to work within? Can you consider a year from now perhaps, two years or are you sufficiently motivated to think about your career shift in terms of months instead? This is all influenced by where you are in the three stages of transition (as outlined in Chapter 1).

➢ What's the **landscape?** – Are you looking after yourself? Are you in the best physical, mental and emotional state to think about your future? How good are you at looking after your health and wellbeing? Most often clients are not as it can be very stressful considering change and we forget to take care of ourselves. I now adopt a checklist using the acronym 'NPALS' (see the 'Love Your N-PALS' section in a few pages time!) when working with my clients. I've found if I make any assumptions about their wellbeing without running through the checklist, we can get bogged down. Nurturing our resilience and wellbeing is vital but can get easily overlooked when we are caught up in our busy lives.

Nurturing Resilience

Changing career direction or just moving jobs can be, as I'm sure you are aware, highly stressful. This itself may not be a bad thing. Reflecting back to the Beckhard Change Equation model, energy and motivation are required to overcome the pain involved in the change. 'Eustress', otherwise known as positive stress, gives us the wherewithal to 'get stuff done' and is a vital source of power in this process. Setting deadlines or milestones, defining goals and getting clear on purpose and vision – these can all incentivise the career change process. When experiencing eustress, we feel excited and that we are able to cope well with the demands placed upon us.

Stress, however, moves into being 'distress' when it interferes with our ability to take action. When the pressure is on-going without respite; when we are required to take on more than we can bear and we start to question our ability to cope, stress becomes the enemy of our search for a new direction. Stress is a well-recognised contributing factor to many serious and chronic illnesses such as cardiovascular disease and depression.

It is vitally important therefore, that we see the value in taking good care of ourselves. It may be tempting to put everything, and everyone else, ahead of our own needs. But without having your needs met and keeping yourself well – in mind and in body - the cumulative effects of trying to navigating a change in direction may well stall you. And at it's worse, you may end up so exhausted you cave in to the familiarities of the 'comfort zone' and give up. For you to really understand the importance of this, let's take a look at the 'Hierarchy of Needs' model, developed by psychologist, Abraham Maslow (1943, 1956) (see Diagram 2 below).

Maslow was interested in understanding how people could fulfil their potential and suggested we are motivated to achieve our needs in a particular hierarchy. Whilst more recent studies have questioned the ordering of this hierarchy, they have supported the concept of universal human needs that have to be met (Tay & Diener, 2011).

The negative effects of stress can interfere with basic *physiological needs* such as our sleeping and eating habits. According to Maslow's 'Hierarchy of Needs' model, such basic needs must be met before we can satisfy other, higher needs. Questioning where and how we are going to earn money actually challenges the next level of needs in this model, *safety and security.*

Love and belonging come next, which include having friends, family and sexual intimacy. This can become compromised from both the stresses involved in trying to work out what to do next with our lives, and the symptoms of being in the confusing 'neutral phase' of transition. We can withdraw from our loved ones; our libido can drop; we may neglect our friendships.

Diagram 2: Maslow's Hierarchy of Needs

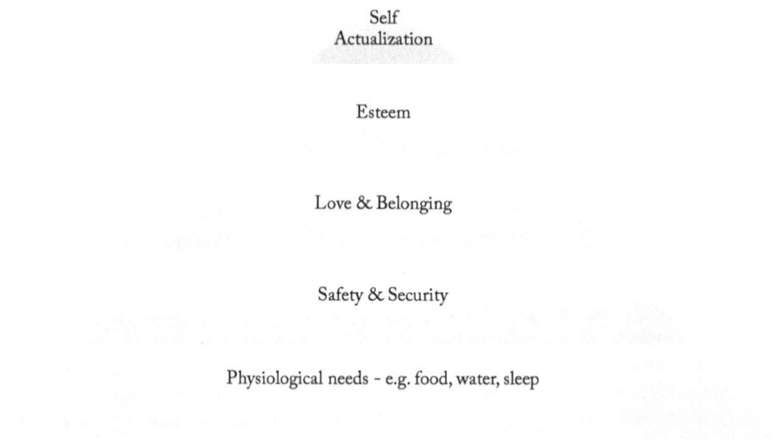

Self
Actualization

Esteem

Love & Belonging

Safety & Security

Physiological needs - e.g. food, water, sleep

(Maslow, 1943, 1954)

Any damage to our experience of a sense of love and belonging affects the next level of needs, *esteem*. Our confidence, sense of achievement, respect for self and others is essential for us to be able to achieve the last set of needs in Maslow's hierarchy, those of *self-actualization*. Maslow saw 'self actualized people' as those who were fulfilled and doing what they were capable of. It is the ability to experience self-actualization that is fundamental for us in 'choosing to flourish'.

Unfortunately, the process of seeking out or responding to change may negatively influence our perception of the extent to which these needs are being met. This may then prevent us from being able to reach self-actualization. The way out of this negative feedback loop is to be *proactive* in nurturing our resilience and wellbeing.

In the Choose2Flourish approach, we focus on ensuring these needs and thus wellbeing are nurtured whilst we move through the 10 steps as outlined in Chapter 5. Indeed I've found with my private clients that it pays to never *assume* people are paying sufficient attention to this. Invariably, there is always more we can be doing to nurture our health and wellbeing that will reap multiple rewards in our career transition.

In terms of supporting a 'resilient and healthy mind', one tool I often apply examines and encourage participants to self-score on a set of 7 'inner and 'outer' factors, taken from the work of David Rock and Dr Daniel Siegel. 'Inner factors' relate to the internally focused activities whilst 'outer factors' are externally found.

'Inner' Factors:

- Sleep

- Downtime

- Altered State

- Focused Attention

'Outer' Factors:

- Physical Activity

- Social Connection

- Play

Good quality sleep - On average adults need 8 hours. It's a myth that sleep can be short changed. You can't 'make up' for its loss by a lie-in at the weekend. Sleep is essential for neuroplasticity to occur, for homeostatic restoration, thermoregulation, tissue repair, immunity, memory, creativity and emotional regulation. We all know what happens after a poor nights sleep! Meeting this basic need is essential.

Down time – (i.e. reflection & relaxation) – this is all about 'intentionally having no intention'. We are in a state of inactivity, doing absolutely nothing that has a predetermined goal; we're 'in the moment', spontaneously doing what emerges. Being in this state allows us to mull over complex issues and can often provide the incubation period that leads to the 'Ah ha!' moments. When we are in 'downtime', the following parts of our brain are activated:

- Medial temporal lobe – memory

- Medial prefrontal cortex – sense of self

- Posterior cingulate – autobiographical reflection

- Lateral parietal cortex – integration.

Altered state – this is an altered state of awareness, where our brain waves go into 'theta' mode. Long-term mindfulness meditation has now been associated with increased attention and emotional regulation, and research suggests there are definite benefits when it comes to preventing and treating depression.

Focused attention – is where we allow our mind to focus on something at 90-minute intervals (the identified optimum time to remain focused). Studies suggest that to support peak performance (and stop ourselves from getting overtired), we should break every 90 minutes for 'PMS' – a pee/ toilet break, some movement or stretching and having a snack or at least a drink of water.

Unfortunately, there is a part of the brain that looks for novelty and we feel a push, usually after only 3 minutes to change activity. Hence the flipping to check emails or phone messages within minutes of sitting down to write that report, for example. It can then take 25 minutes for us to get focused once more on the task in hand. This leads to significant depletion of energy levels (our pre-frontal cortex is very energy demanding), running the risk of leaving us feeling exhausted by the end of the day. Given that we need energy to drive our will power (also centred in the prefrontal cortex), it is perhaps not surprising therefore that those who fail to manage their attention in this way struggle to undertake the actions they know they ought to take as part of this process of navigating transition and career change.

Physical activity – adults need to partake in regular, moderate physical activity, roughly 30 minutes a day, 5 days of the week, to maintain our health. Medical research has made the link between the lack of physical activity and poor health very clear. Being sedentary increases the risk of almost every lifestyle disease, including heart attack and stroke. Being active also 'feels' good. As in play, our 'feel good' hormones are released (see below).

Play – Play activates joy in our basic emotional system. Joyful play stimulates the reward centres in our brain and dopamine; a 'feel-good' hormone, amongst others, is released. Play stimulates the creation of new neural pathways as we think more creatively and activate different memories. Play is often a social activity (see social connection), and facilitates learning in both adults and children. Play dampens down the release of cortisol and the stress response.

Social connection – human beings need to connect with others from early life and this remains an important source of safety. We have a need to feel 'seen' and acknowledged by others. This all combines to give us a sense of experiencing security. There are multiple benefits to social contact and the lack of social contact is perceived as 'threat' and our brain reacts accordingly.

Deepak Chopra and Rudolph E. Tanzi in their book 'Super Brain', (2013) consider that most of us are failing to nurture our 'inner world' by spending most of our time on 'focused activity' at work, coming home and then trying to find a way to relax and distracting ourselves (through TV, gaming, Facebook) until its time for bed. With no regular time set aside for self-reflection or meditation, our brain has little chance to rest. We can get chaotic or confused inside, unable to find clarity and peace of mind. Rigidity in our thinking and behaviour patterns may be established as a result. <u>Not</u> what we want when we're trying to progress through our transition into a new job or career!

In the Choose2Flourish approach, we also assess an 8th factor in this tool, that of self-efficacy.

Self-efficacy – the ability to believe you can do it, that you're able to trust in yourself and accomplish things. 'Locus of control' provides a useful measure of this and you can access a short quiz that will show you where you are on the scale of high external to high internal locus of control on my website by going to www.choose2flourish.co.uk/lcquiz

Look After Your N-PALS

Another way the Choose2Flourish approach supports resilience and well-being, is through encouraging participants to consider and self-score themselves on the acronym, N-PALS. No matter what your aim or intention is on the programme or where you›re starting from, if you are not looking after your ‹N-PALS›, you›re not going to succeed.

Simply put, 'N-PALS' are the nutrients in the ground in which you plant your tree. Just as you won›t expect a strong oak tree to grow from infertile soil, so you can›t expect to flourish when these fundamentals are weak or missing.

N - Nutrition - A healthy plate is in fact one half vegetables! And we do need a variety, to 'eat a rainbow' every day. Most people know that eating too many calories can lead to being an unhealthy body weight but in recent years, the damaging effects specifically associated with excess sugar in our diet is increasingly being recognised, both on our physical and mental health. Being aware of *what* we are eating and taking steps to ensure we are eating healthily is an important supportive activity in any transition.

PA - Physical Activity - 30 minutes a day, 5 times a week, 10,000 steps every day. Most of us don't do enough. And even if we are meeting cardiovascular requirements, chances are we're missing out on the weight bearing exercises or the stretching (vital especially for the ‹maturing› body.)

L - Love - including **Self-Love** - Do you show compassion to yourself? Do you nurture positive thoughts and allow yourself not to be perfect? We all fail or let people down sometimes. We can say the wrong thing. It's human. Learn, yes, grow, of course, but first and foremost, be kind to yourself.

S - Sleep – most adults need 8 hours a night. No electronic devices in the bedroom, clear the clutter and create a calm, *sleeping* environment.

It's not rocket science. It's often the things we want to jump over in order to get to the more exciting stuff. But putting the effort into ensuring you have fertile soil from which to grow, your N-PALS will give you the energy and healthy, sustainable habits to enable you to reach your goals and attain your vision. These elements need time and attention. However, remember this. These nutrients and the 'inner' and 'outer' factors described in nurturing resilience do not on their own lead you to thriving in your career, to living a flourishing life. To quote Chopra (2013):

" Nutrients do not create meaning. They don't define a vision or set a long-range goal. Those are your tasks as a reality maker. "

Establishing and finding meaning, vision and purpose are all key aspects of the Choose2Flourish approach.

The 10 Steps

In the next chapter we move to consider in detail the 10-steps that make up the Choose to Flourish approach to changing career and thriving in life. These steps have been developed through the work I do with private clients and those who choose to work with me in a group format.

You can choose to join a '**Choose2Flourish VIP Intensive**' where we spend a powerful day going through the 10-steps, interwoven with additional material that builds participants confidence and clarity around their vision and direction.

Alternatively, there is the '**Choose2Flourish**' **Mastermind Programme**, a 6 month course, that leads participants through the 10 Steps, enabling them to remain in their 'stretch zone' as they work through their career change and manage the stresses associated with such transition. We also have a lot of fun and laughter along the way. Just because this is about your direction and purpose in life, doesn't mean to say it has to feel 'heavy' and can't be enjoyable!

The 10 Steps explored in the next chapter are:

Step 1: Take Stock – of the facts and emotions relating to your current reality;

Step 2: Let Go – of what needs to go;

Step 3: Know What You Need and Enjoy (Flourishing Compass, Part I);

Step 4: Find Your Strengths and Will (Flourishing Compass, Part II);

Step 5: Pin Point Your Location – building on Step 1;

Step 6: Identify a Destination – to activate your passion and desire;

Step 7: Consistently Take Simple Steps of Inspiring Action;

Step 8: Actively Manage an Empowering Mind-set – for self-belief;

Step 9: Check Your Bearings – as things can shift as you go along;

Step 10: Trust in Your New Beginning – recognising when you're there.

To give you an idea of the *impact* following these steps can have, presented below are some testimonials from clients who attended a recent Choose2Flourish VIP Intensive.

"Before attending the VIP day with Rhian I was scared and unable to move towards my goal because it felt too big a thing to achieve. Over the course of the day I was able to identify and break down the different components that will help me achieve my overall goal. Now I know what steps I have to take and am more confident and trusting in my own ability. I feel I can conquer the world and anything is possible! I highly recommend doing this because it brings so much clarity and closure on the past and helps set achieveable goals. Rhian is a joy to work with – Thanks Rhian!" Esther Small

"Prior to the C2F VIP day I was lacking in confidence and clarity to make the next step professionally. Over the day I learnt to breakdown perceived barriers into manageable chunks and create a vision for myself. Now I'm ready to take that first small step, map and compass in hand! I highly recommend this day to those in periods of professional transition"

Kai Barnes

Overview of the Choose2Flourish Approach

➢ It is normal to feel fear when contemplating change so find ways that build your courage to overcome those fears and prevent you from slipping into your panic zone.

➢ Switch off the sat nav and tune into using your own map and compass instead.

➢ Navigate your external change and internal transition by developing your inner compass, your 'Flourishing Compass'.

➢ Build your map by first considering it's landscape and scale – what's your timescale? How are you physically, mentally and emotionally?

➢ Look after yourself at all times – think about your N-PALS.

➢ Spend time on each of the 10 steps, working at a pace that feels right for you.

➢ Get support – share your journey with trusted friends and loved ones, a professional coach or mastermind group for a successful transition and career change.

— 59 —

CHAPTER 5

The Ten Steps to Successful Transition

These steps are presented here in the order you should ideally work through. However, for some people a different order may feel more appropriate – just make sure all steps are covered. Some steps may need more reflection than others. You may feel you have nothing to let go of (Step 2), but if you start to stall in taking action at Step 7, come back and think again. Take your time. Like making a good cup of tea, give things time to brew. Offered amongst the steps are a few case studies and some personal anecdotes. See how these relate back to your own situation and apply or set aside as you see fit.

Remember to consider where you are in the 3 stages of transition. If you're right in the middle of the chaotic neutral zone, working on the first 5 steps is going to feel easier than the others. Go with that. Be aware that any 'new beginning' invariable has a few false starts, a couple of dead ends. Working through the 'Choose to Flourish' process is certainly going to help you avoid some of them but not all. It's part of the natural process. See yourself as the hero or heroine in the middle of the adventure! As the creator of your story, it's your adventure. Just remember: You're in charge of writing the ending.

Step 1: Take Stock

The unexamined life is not worth living

Socrates

Effective explorers, the ones who make the journey and come home to tell the tale, go prepared. It's no good *assuming* that the route out will take 5 days, taking food for 7 and finding out too late that it's going to need 10 days, minimum. You'll get very hungry, end up with a very unhappy team and possible make some very bad errors of judgement that could lead to disaster. There is no such thing as perfect knowledge and as such, we often need to make a judgement call which requires, in the first instance, an **assessment of the facts**.

On leaving Oxford University I had the pleasure and privilege of being part of a University Expedition to Northern Pakistan. We got the Royal Geographical Society's seal of approval (which meant we'd done our planning!) and set off to explore the upper reaches of Shimshal, in the Karakorum Mountains in North Pakistan. We were following in the footsteps of renowned explorer, Ernest Shackleton who had once mapped these hidden valleys and mountains, apart from one tantalizing gap that he left on his map. We were going to fill that gap. Eventually after weeks of trekking and a few 15,000ft passes, we got ourselves into the massive Shaksgam valley, the fault-created geo-political border between China and Pakistan, and our destination. Once the mapping was done, we faced a choice. Do we try to walk out via China (we had the visas) or retrace our steps?

We took stock. How were our food reserves (low), morale (high), and health? (mixed – a lot of tummy trouble) How far would it be to the next likely village and a chance to replenish supplies? We couldn't take the risk of relying on our assumptions. We went by the facts. We retraced our steps – and got back home.

The same needs to apply to your career crossroads. Exploring the realities of your current situation is a vital first step. With the help of a trusted friend or professional coach, lay out the facts one by one. Look for and check your evidence. Try to avoid being judgemental or critical of yourself.

Case Study: Transitioning into Self-Employment

Stuart wanted to leave his fulltime job to focus on his ambitions to be a personal trainer. Despite considerable commitment and motivation he had a lot of fears around being self-employed which kept pushing him into 'panic zone' resulting in him 'freezing' and being unable to take any meaningful action that would bring him closer to his goal. When we went back to check for hidden assumptions we found that he had assumed his current place of work would not tolerate him working part time.

This assumption was preventing him from seeking out a half step, that is, of working part-time in a paid role whilst he explored and set up his own business. This was very important to Stuart as he had a strong value and need around security and 'flying solo' without any backup was too much of a leap for him. We go into 'panic zone' when the actions we're trying to take are too big a step, causing high levels of anxiety and an inability to progress.

By checking out the facts, by taking stock of the *realities* of the situation (and not relying solely on his own *assumptions,* Stuart was able to see a way forward. In fact, this turned out to be a very positive step blessing as through it, he came to shift perspective and see what he really wanted was a portfolio career – being an employee for half the week (which met his need for security) and self-employed for the rest (allowing him to follow his dreams and need for some creativity and autonomy).

What's the **evidence t**o say you are at a career crossroads / need to change direction? What is real about what's going on? Spot the assumptions you are making (this can be hard, hence an external perspective can usefully assist). It might help to think about:

- ➤ What you like and dislike about what you do
- ➤ How you feel, clearly stated
- ➤ Future prospects
- ➤ The people
- ➤ The politics
- ➤ Your family situation
- ➤ Your work life balance
- ➤ Where your priorities lie (where do you spend your time?)
- ➤ What's missing

Something has brought you to read this book. Explore, by identifying the facts, what that is. Whilst emotions are a very good indicator of what is going on inside us, try to find the real reasons behind the emotion rather than just stopping at for example, 'I'm really frustrated with my boss'. Go deeper. "I'm really frustrated with my boss as she never lets me go with my ideas. This makes me feel that my skills are not valued. Feeling valued and using my skills are very important to me".

Taking stock is also about *getting clear on your financial parameters,* as explored in Chapter 4. What are your numbers around your salary or monthly income? Whilst we know this is far from being the defining point in your search, having this grounding in figures is illuminating. For example, not believing you can make money from what you really want to do is a common stumbling block to achieving that purposeful career. However, how can you *know* that if you don't have a clear handle on how much you need to live off in the first place? Don't be an ostrich with your head in the sand around this. Track your spending over a month or two, work out your sums and set financial parameters.

Tip: Check your facts: What's real and what are you assuming? What do your *emotions* tell you about what is really going on? If you have difficulty doing this yourself, seek out support to help you separate fact from fiction and to identify what your feelings are *really* saying.

Step 2: Let Go

The key to change – is to let go of fear

Rosanne Cash

In the blockbuster Disney film 'Frozen', one of the lead female characters, Elsa, sings a highly memorable song "Let it Go'. Love it or hate it (the song prompts rather strong reactions in many people), it's a powerful rejection by this character of everything she has had to put up with in her life, living as she does with magical powers that can turn everything into ice and snow. The moral of the story is simple - don't let fear rule your world, let love in instead – echoing what most spiritual leaders, personal development gurus, thought leaders (as well as some songwriters) say.

In working through Step 1 of this guide you're going to revisit situations you may regret. It is a normal aspect of being human to get caught up in thoughts such as 'I wish I'd done that, said this'. You can easily find yourself thinking 'I should have pushed for, stopped that, and made my move then'. Whilst this can develop the motivation for action and change (remember the Change Equation; the discomfort of the present, alongside the vision of the future must overcome pain involved in changing), if we allow ourselves to keep re-visiting such regrets and disappointments, it's going to become harder for us to fruitfully progress into whatever is coming next.

For many people 'letting go' can be the hardest thing. Our thoughts create neural patterns inside our brains by neurons 'firing' together and getting 'wired in' to a sequence of thought. Changing our thoughts is the vital first step in changing our behaviour but it requires repetition and persistence. If we're caught up in regret, we're focusing our effort on maintaining those negative thought patterns and neural pathways. This holds us back from achieving what it is we're seeking.

As we've explored in the previous chapters, managing a successful transition in our life requires us to make a good 'ending' to what has gone on before. As in any successful organisational change management programme, we need to acknowledge in ourselves what is coming to an end and what we have to be letting go of, in order to allow ourselves to move into the next stage of our lives and careers. This could include a sense of loss over leaving familiar colleagues or a work culture you've really enjoyed. We need to recognise what we have learnt and allow ourselves to start a new chapter in our lives by consciously choosing to 'let go' of unhelpful, circular thoughts and behaviours.

In Chapter 6 we explore some of the barriers that can crop up, sabotaging and blocking your desire to move on in your working life. The biggest cluster of blockers is around fear. Often our imagined fears will freeze us more readily than what is actually real. As such, we must illuminate the things we are finding scary about switching career direction or changing jobs, and one by one, work through them all, challenging our beliefs around those fears and finding ways to manage them. This is often a hard thing to do but it needs to be done. By letting go we create a space of possibility for new things to come in.

One point to finish with here is this. Sometimes we can be tempted to skip through this step as we don't believe we've got anything significant to let go of. However we may find that as we move further into the process, we get stuck. We find ourselves procrastinating. We believe we are motivated enough to take the actions we say we'll do but then weeks, months later, nothing has happened. If that happens to you, come back to this step and look again at what you need to let go of. I promise there will be something that you need to close down, end, let go.

Tip: Explore what it is you need to let go off before you can move on. What needs to end? Acknowledge the learning those disappointments and regrets have provided and then consciously choose to let them go.

Step 3: Know What You Need and Enjoy

Are you doing what you are truly capable of or have you chosen the path of least resistance?

When we know ourselves deeply and have trust in our decisions, we are far more likely to choose a route through our working lives that brings us meaning, accomplishment, good relationships, engagement and positive emotions – in other words the ability to flourish! Without self-confidence, we cannot flourish, which is why I wrote my first book, 'Alchemy for the Mind: Create Your Confident Core'. In developing the Flourishing Compass tool as part of the Choose2Flourish programme, I wanted to provide a simple way for clients to work out key elements that build self-awareness, self-confidence and ultimately, intuition. The following is our starting point for working with this tool.

The Flourishing Compass

North – what do you **need?** What is important to you to have in your career?

In answering this, we need to reflect on our **values.** Values are the principles by which we live our life, our accepted standards. They help us make the distinction between right and wrong, good and bad. Our driving or operational values are single, abstract words that have meaning and importance, give us focus and direction, principles and standards. Understanding our values helps us to understand our natural motivations. When it comes to our careers, it is vitally important that we know what values need to be met. For example, values such as security, autonomy, power, financial reward, creativity, meaning, impact and status.

Once you are clear as to what values need to be met in your career, the next step is to assess how they are being met right now. Identify what is missing. On a scale of 1 to 10, when 10 is completely present and 1 is not present at all, score how you are experiencing these values in your life, in your work. What needs to change in order for you to increase those scores?

Often the very first things we list as our values here are not really the most important ones. We need to dig a little deeper in order to tap into the key drivers. Asking yourself, what does having x (the value you've stated) give me? Often how you answer that is the more important, underlying value that needs to be met.

East – what do you **enjoy?** What gets you '**into flow**'?

For many people, enjoying their work is not something they've necessarily given a lot of attention to. If we 'fall into' a career and end up on a certain path because we're **good at something**, we may not have stopped to consider whether or not we *like* doing what we're good at.

This was something I've personally struggled with at times. I'm good at organising things, have a reputation with my friends for being the one who makes things happen. I've organised numerous large-scale conferences and events. I can project plan, develop a critical path and move mountains to ensure success – but do I like doing that event management? No, I don't, not really. It's stressful and doesn't give me a lasting sense of accomplishment once the immediate relief that it's all over has passed. In spite of knowing this about myself, because I am good at it, I do occasionally find myself slipping back into doing such activities. However I'm getting better at delegating the detail and giving myself *permission* not to get dragged back in.

'Flow' has been the subject of considerable research in the field of positive psychology. One leading researcher, Mikaly Csikszentmihalyi states that flow is "the state in which people are so involved in an activity that nothing else seems to matter" (Flow, 1991). We go into flow best when we use our strengths – see the next point on our Flourishing Compass.

Since becoming an author I've realized, to my considerable joy, that I love writing and reach a state of flow typing away on my computer. I enjoy being a coach and a trainer as well, but as both those activities require me to be mindful of and managing my time, it is in writing that I find that flow - and my life is now considerably richer than it was before.

'E' in this Flourishing Compass can also be used to examine '**Energy.**' We have to manage our energy levels if we are going to successfully navigate a career change. The inner work of transition, and the outer work of seeking change, places increasing demands on ourselves. Sometimes the enormity of what we are trying to do and the state of the world around us, can drag us back into losing hope and belief. If we look out for ways in which we can nourish our energy, we place ourselves in a far stronger position to keep going on our journey.

We go into this some more in Chapter 6 and again in the Choose2Flourish Mastermind Programme and VIP Intensive Days. For those of you who know this is a considerable barrier to you moving forwards, I whole-heartedly recommend Nicky Marshall's '**Discover Your Bounce**' programme, www.discoveryourbounce.com

Tip: Find your 'North, identify your 'East'. Don't stop exploring this until you're certain you've got to the real core of what matters.

Case Study: What drives us may not be what we think.

Working with Ben as he looked to change jobs, we spent some time examining the values that were behind his career choices to date. Ben was the CEO of a small charity and his first child was on the way. Whilst some may think to sit tight in such a situation, Ben knew he had reached a point of stagnation in the role he was doing and re-aligning his career before he became a father made sense to him.

One thing Ben was struggling with was whether or not he was cut out to be a CEO. On the one hand, he enjoyed the decision making and leadership this provided him but on the other, he missed a certain amount of creativity and the 'hands on' element from when he was less senior. He toyed with the idea of aspiring to a less demanding role (especially as he recognised the challenges ahead becoming a dad).

When we explored his values and motivations however, it was absolutely clear that having 'power' was a critical factor for him. A leadership role was vital and he would be unlikely to stay very satisfied and engaged for long if his next role didn't offer that.

At first Ben was rather uncomfortable with this, having some unhelpful beliefs around what power meant and what the types of people in power were like. Once we had unpicked those unhelpful beliefs and assumptions and Ben got to realise how these were sabotaging him, he became very comfortable knowing this about himself. Whilst his subsequent new job wasn't a CEO position, he did ensure there was sufficient autonomy and leadership present for him to enjoy and thrive in that position.

Step 4: Find Your Strengths and Your Will

Everyone has a talent – it's a matter of moving around until you find it

George Lucas

Knowing what you need and what you enjoy are the first two points of your 'Flourishing Compass'. In the **Choose2Flourish Mastermind Program** we delve into this in more detail and consider a few other aspects but what's described previously is a very powerful starting point with this tool. We now move onto working out your South and your West.

South - what are your **strengths**?

In the Choose2Flourish approach, we make an important distinction here between your 'skills' and 'strengths'. Skills are what you are good at. Strengths are what you are good at – and enjoy! This helps keep us focused on those aspects that are most conducive to us flourishing.

As many of you reading this will probably appreciate, acknowledging what we are good at is difficult for many people. We're far more likely to remember the stuff we don't do so well whilst experiencing amnesia over the great things we've actually achieved and enjoy doing. This is all down to our evolution, as focusing on where we need to improve helped us to evolve as a species. Today, an awareness of our strengths is hugely beneficial and when it comes to navigating our careers, essential.

If you know and consciously use aspects of yourself you are good at, you'll feel more positive. This in itself brings about real benefits in a beautiful positive feedback loop. For example, when we are able to use and apply our strengths, we're able to think more expansively and more creatively, as explored by Barbara Fredrickson (2009) in her 'broaden and build' theory of positive emotions. This now well-accepted theory states that positivity opens our minds, making us more receptive and more creative, whilst enabling us to build new skills, new knowledge and new ways of being. Using our strengths in work allows us to show and grow our competence, enhancing our confidence and allowing us to flourish.

As well as using this awareness to identify those roles and areas where you are able to use more of your strengths, every day, you can apply this directly to your search for a new career direction. As we explore in Step 7, once you know where you are and where you'd like to go, taking action is vital. How to best go about this, however, means identifying those actions that are both aligned to who you are and *play to your strengths*. For example, for some who are confident and well connected, that might mean directly contacting people who are currently in the roles they aspire to through using their network on LinkedIn. For the technology savvy, this might mean creating a short video post, a v-log, which can be used as part of a resumé.

Knowing what your strengths are can also help you be aware of your 'shadow' side. This is the opposite, unhelpful aspect of having that strength. For example, 'a love of excellence' has a shadow of being a perfectionist; 'optimism, zest and energy for life' (one of mine) can also lead you to overcommitting, so you need to take a few reality checks. Transactional Analysis (a theory of communication) frames someone's character traits you may find annoying as a 'strength overdone'. Developing insights as to where you (and others) are perhaps overdoing some strengths can lead to better relationships, at work, at home, with friends, family and colleagues. It can also help you understand where you might self-sabotage when it comes to changing career or moving into a new job. For example, a love of learning when 'overdone' could mean seeking to get qualifications when you don't really need to, or putting off making decisions until you've read about and learnt everything you think you need to know.

How do you know what your strengths are? You are probably aware of some, but identifying your strengths can be tricky (partly due of course to our innate tuning into the negative and the difficulty we all have in recognising what we are truly good at!) One way is to ask yourself what strengths you have just used when you have done something you feel good about. If you have a friend or trusted colleague who you feel can give you honest feedback (itself a real skill), you can also try asking them, or you could work with a coach or find a Mastermind programme to support you in doing this.

West – where is your **will**?

As we discovered in earlier chapters, there is a certain amount of inertia and fear that needs to be overcome or managed in order to navigate change, particularly where big external shifts are required along with the internal transition. Exploring our motivations and identifying our desire is essential for us to then determine and nurture the willpower required to keep us moving along and achieving our goal.

For example, in order to write my first book, I realised I needed to make changes to my working hours. I couldn't find the time nor focus during the normal working day so I realised I needed to wake up earlier and write for a few hours before the children got up and required my attention. That was okay for a few days but then I realised I was flagging and it was going to be hard to keep the effort going. In order to 'find that effort', I explored my motivations. Why did I want to write this book about confidence? Who was going to benefit if it got published? How would I benefit from seeing 'Alchemy for the Mind' in print?

Using one of my strengths (writing), I wrote out all the reasons why I was doing it, answering the Why, Who and How questions above. Once it was all out on paper, I condensed it down into one short sentence and pinned it on the wall above my desk, with another copy above the bathroom sink and also as the screensaver on my phone. I'd followed the exact same process when setting up my coaching business. This belief statement still looks down from my wall at me today, reminding me that "I commit to building a thriving a sustainable business that positively transforms peoples lives and helps create a flourishing world". *Regularly reading* those statements reminds me of my will, my intentions and helps keep me positive, focused and on track when obstacles arise and my willpower flags.

What can you do to identify your motivations and intentions? By what means can you nurture sufficient willpower to keep you moving? You may find identifying inspiring quotes and pictures that resonate with you helpful here. If your vision for the future is clear (Step 6), then in addition to a belief statement such as the example I gave above, creating a vision board with pictures, quotes and statements that define that vision can be very powerful. Many of my clients in the Choose2Flourish Programme don't have a clear vision at the start of the process so we often create a vision board at this point that covers the broad things they want and are motivated by.

In building your 'Flourishing Compass' as outlined in Steps 3 and 4 in this 10-step guide, you have created a simple means to understand your inner motivations, values, strengths and desires. When these aspects of your inner world are familiar and trusted, you will find it easier to work out exactly where you currently are and where you'd like to go, (Steps 5 and 6 in this guide).

Tip: Explore your strengths with a trusted friend, colleague or coach. Actively use your strengths to shape how you approach your career change. Be mindful of where you may be 'overdoing it' as this can sabotage your chances of success. Identify your motivations and be proactive in keeping your desires alive. Willpower, centred in the prefrontal cortex of our brains, requires a lot of energy so don't expect too much of yourself all the time. Write out a positive statement that best sums up your intentions and read it, every day, to nurture your willpower.

Step 5: Pin Point Your Location

Some people seem to have such a good sense of direction that on emerging from a subway or metro, they head off in exactly the right direction. I'm not one of those people. Before I accepted this fact (it's taken a few years), I would invariably stride off in exactly the wrong direction. I would have studied a map before setting off, even checked at the station but would still find myself going wrong. I now have a new approach. I do all my checks, go to walk out the way I think I need to go - and then make myself stop and check I'm where I should be. Almost always I need to turn around and go the other way...

The point I'm, making is this. You need to know exactly **where you are** in order to know where it is you want to go. Sometimes it's not obvious where you are and to determine this, you need to look a little deeper.

This step builds on what we have already explored in Steps 1,2, 3 and 4. It helps to be aware of what your locus of control is, internal or external, as that shapes your attitude. You can discover your locus of control by coming to my website and doing a simple quiz – visit <u>www. choose2flourish.co.uk/lcquiz</u>.

Reflecting on where you are in the 3 stages of transition – the ending, neutral zone or new beginning – is also important.

The following questions are designed to trigger your thinking here. You may come up with some more of your own. Build on what you now know about yourself to explore your answers in more depth.

What do you want to take with you?

What do you want to leave behind?

Where are you? (in stages of transition, in the 'novelty to mastery' cycle)

How are you?

- Emotionally

- Physically

- Spiritually

- Energetically

- Mentally

What would 10 out of 10 look like for you in each of these areas?

Score each area, with ten being the highest/ couldn't be better.

What does that tell you?

Tip: Think as widely and as deeply as you can here. Be honest with your feelings. Try not to be self-critical. Things are what they are. You have the capacity to make things better.

Step 6: Identify A Destination

All successful people, men and women, are big dreamers. They imagine what their future could be, ideal in every respect, and then they work every day toward their distant vision, that goal or purpose.

Brian Tracy

There's an important choice of words made in the title of this step. I could have said 'identify *your* destination' but I've deliberately used 'identify *a* destination' instead. Read the two phrases again now. Can you see why I chose the latter?

'A destination' suggests somewhere you want to head to. It may not be 'the' 100% perfect or ultimate destination, but it is somewhere you know you *do* want to reach. 'Your destination' is different. It suggests there is only one, perfect place for you to go. Not only can that create an enormous amount of pressure (you've got to get this *right* for goodness sake!) but also it suggests a false premise. You may have a clear sense of where you want to be heading in your career but then again you may not. If you think you've got to find the perfect solution, the likelihood is you'll be triggered into panic zone and as we know, nothing productive happens when you're in there. Also, what appears right and true for you just now could well shift, as you get closer to something else that you then focus your attention on achieving.

This is a step that many people can stumble over when working on their own through their career change and associated transition. I've often observed clients initially struggle with this as there can be powerful sabotaging beliefs at work that prevent them from creating a powerful vision of where they would like to go. For example:

- ➤ They are scared to fail, so don't allow themselves to have a vision in the first place. If you don't have anything to measure yourself by, you can't fail!

- ➤ They don't believe they deserve to be happier/ wealthier/ more valued/ more satisfied than they are right now.

- ➤ They haven't let themselves look that far ahead into the future, believing it's somehow 'unlucky' to do so.

- ➤ They feel it's basically wrong to want or expect more from their life. They should accept what they are given.

- ➤ They can only think about what they *don't* want rather than what they *do* want as they've never done that before.

- ➤ They're scared about what their partner/ friends/ family will think.

- ➤ They're scared that they don't have what it takes to get them to where they dream of going

This is why finding and activating courage is a key part of the Choose2Flourish approach. We need to find our *courage* to overcome these initial fears so that we can allow ourselves some quality 'dreamtime'. If we keep pushing at developing our vision without acknowledging, and working through, what is preventing us from moving forwards, we're going to get frustrated and quite possibly give up. We can help ourselves here by reflecting on situations where we've overcome something difficult in our past. By finding evidence of how and where we've been courageous, we can help ourselves see what we need to do now to progress.

Sometimes we need to give ourselves *permission* to spend time reflecting on our vision and personal dreams. If, on reading the list above you found much to relate to, you will find working with a professional coach on an individual basis or in a mastermind programme, very helpful indeed.

Tip: Set aside some quality time to explore what your personal vision is. How do you want your life to be in 5 or 10 years time? How do you want to show up in that vision? Sometimes it helps to put a bit of distance between now and this desired future in order to overcome the fear and blocks mentioned above. You can try doing this by writing a letter to a close friend, a year or 5 years from now, celebrating all the great things that have happened to bring you into this vision.

Without vision, the people perish

Proverbs 29:18

Step 7: Consistently Take Small Steps of Inspiring Action

Make resolutions with yourself and do them. This has a huge impact on your own self-respect and self esteem, your self-efficacy and belief.

Brian Tracy

Setting inspiring goals, writing them down and reviewing them on a regular basis are essential actions for you to realise your dreams. Keeping those aspirations inside your head, even if you've planned out a few steps, does not do it! Researchers who followed a group of Harvard students in the 1970's discovered that the small minority who did have goals and wrote them down (c. 3%), were far more successful in their lives than the majority of their classmates who didn't.

In addition to writing them down, goals should be discussed with a trusted friend or confidant. Whether you are best motivated by being held accountable, or by being able to celebrate your steps forward through rewarding yourself, having someone with whom to share your innermost aspirations is going to be incredibly helpful. **Choose2Flourish Mastermind Programme** participants really benefit in this respect. Not only do they have access to expert coaching, they also receive the collective wisdom of the group, all of whom are going through similar experiences of change and transition as they navigate a shift to a new career direction. They are held accountable, challenged and supported – a powerful and productive mix.

Whilst all of the above are crucial, the **most** important thing is making sure you **align your goals with your values.** You might think that is obvious, but so many people pursue goals they think they **should** aspire to, not necessarily the ones that call out from their hearts, hoping to be heard. Think back on your 'North' in your Flourishing Compass. How does what you're planning to do meet those needs, match those values?

Some people are more resistant than most to the opinions of other people, of the prevailing 'social norm'. Others are less so. If you are 'hard wired' to avoid conflict, to want security and please others, working out exactly what you want can be rather tricky. I know - it's taken me several decades to get clear on who I am and want I truly want. We are all influenced to some degree by our parents' expectations of us, by our teachers and early environment. Sometimes this can be incredibly helpful, sometimes less so – or indeed, in some cases, downright toxic.

Learning to listen and trust what is true for you, whilst possibly a difficult journey, is worth the effort.

So how do you know if you are heading in the right direction? How can you best check that the goals you are setting for yourself truly match what your heart desires and your purpose in life? One tool that clients have found very useful in this respect is what I call the '**head, heart, gut check**'.

After exploring your options for action and identifying which actions you're planning to take, ask your 'head' what it thinks of it and note the answer that comes up inside. Then ask your 'heart', again noting the answer. Finally ask your 'stomach' the same question. Between the logical response from your head, the emotional feeling from your heart and the quiet, gut instinct, you will know whether or not you're aligning your actions.

Tip: Outline small, simple action steps to begin with. Build up from a base of wins rather than 'shooting for the moon' which is more likely to result in failure, which will shake your confidence. Movement creates confidence – inaction breeds doubt. There is a balance to be struck between moving too fast, and failing to check your alignment and moving too slowly, getting disheartened and stopping.

Your work is to discover your work and then with all your heart to give yourself to it

Buddha

Step 8: Actively Manage an Empowering Mind-Set

Man often becomes what he believes himself to be.

Mahatma Gandhi

We all need to believe in ourselves to achieve anything of importance to us in life but this is especially so when we are contemplating, or progressing through, a significant life change, such as seeking a new career direction. Even after we have made a move, we still need to be aware of how important it is to nurture an empowering mind-set. Change challenges us like nothing else. As we move from novelty to mastery of our situation (remember the 7 year cycle mentioned earlier), and navigate our way through the internal transition process, developing the tools and strategies that nurture a supportive inner dialogue is invaluable.

In an excellent, and much quoted book entitled 'Think and Grow Rich' by Napoleon Hill, he states:

'Whatever the mind can conceive and believe, the mind can achieve…. regardless of how many times you may have failed in the past or how lofty your aims or hopes may be".

Belief is an essential aspect of finding your way into a new role or career. Definitions of 'belief' vary slightly but pick up the combination of having both confidence and trust present; **self-belief is therefore having the confidence and trust in yourself that you will prevail**.

There is a very important distinction to be made here between *imagining* yourself somewhere new and *believing* yourself to be there. Some people struggle, of course, with the imagining part, which we covered in Step 6. However if you can imagine it but you <u>don't</u> truly believe it, then you will still not be able to achieve it. Your worry, doubt and uncertainty will act as a barrier that will stop you from making the leap, or consistently taking those small steps of inspired action (Step 7).

Unfortunately even those with high levels of self-belief (and a high internal locus of control) may find this gets eroded or misplaced for a range of reasons, such as:

> Working with people who cannot see your strengths and

value;

> A series of mishaps, false starts or apparent errors in your judgement;

> Loss of confidence in your competence, perhaps after having a baby or time off work due to illness;

> Overly critical and unsupportive parents or significant others during and since your childhood;

> Experiencing poor line management ranging from the incompetent, to exploitative, or bullying;

> Experiencing poor leadership;

> Taking a 'make do' job and finding you're unable to use your skills and natural preferences;

> Failing examinations or poor performance at school, university, or in seeking professional qualifications;

> Not having basic needs, such as physiological, safety, love and belonging met (see Maslow's Hierarchy of Needs as discussed in Chapter 4);

> Feeling unable to effect change around you as it's part of something way beyond your level of control.

Recognising the situations, environments and/or people that drain your self-belief is an important starting point to creating more belief in yourself. **What do you need to stop or start doing here?**

There is a very popular saying in the personal development world which you may well have heard. It says **"Energy flows where the focus goes"**. So many clients and participants on my programmes start off by only being able to state what they *don't* want in their life. Linked to that are all the reasons why they believe they *won't* be successful including the barriers that are getting in their way. If that had remained their guiding mind-set then it would have been a struggle to help them find and follow their new path forwards.

Mind-set is such a crucial issue that while we touch upon it in many of the other steps in this process, it is included as a separate step here to ensure actions are taken to nurture positive and empowering self-belief.

Focusing on **why** we will be successful, why we will have the career, the life of our dreams, is a powerful way of 're-setting' ourselves to have such vital self-belief. To help with this, look for evidence from your past to tell you *why you will get there* this time round.

Changing a negative or limiting belief around the desired change first requires the negative thoughts to be acknowledged. Once awareness has been raised, the focus shifts to consciously changing that to instead be a positive thought – which gets repeated, often. Examples of possible negative thoughts transformed into affirmations are:

- ➢ 'I'm too old to change my career direction' becomes '*I am the perfect age to find purposeful work*'.

- ➢ 'No-one will hire me' could become '*I offer a unique package of expertise and skills that are valued by my new employer*'.

- ➢ 'I don't have what it takes to change career' can become '*I offer the perfect combination that will attract the right opportunities to me*'.

This takes effort and persistence as stopping the negativity can be challenging as in effect we are re-wiring the brain! This needs to then be followed up with action that pushes people from their comfort zone and into 'stretch' (but not 'panic').

Sometimes deep-seated beliefs can't be shifted by trying to re-wire through mantras, affirmations and positive action. Other tools, such as Emotional Freedom Technique (or Tapping) may offer a different way forward if that's the case.

And finally on this step; when working on self-beliefs, the impact of the affirmations, such as the ones suggested above, can be amplified if an associated positive *feeling* is also created inside. This may mean using a memory of when you've done something similar and all has gone well, or imagining it if no memory is to hand. Whatever means is used, repeatedly generating a powerful feeling inside linked to *believing* yourself in the place you want to be is a highly effective way of controlling any self-doubt and fear that can attempt to sabotage your concerted efforts for a successful transition. We come back to this point again in Chapter 6, but as Dale Carnegie says, pro-actively finding ways that build confidence also helps create the evidence required to support an empowering and supportive mind-set.

Inaction breeds fear and doubt. Action breeds confidence and courage. Go out and get busy.

Dale Carnegie

Step 9: Check Your Bearings

So you've got going. You've used your compass in Steps 3 and 4 to get clear on what you need, what you enjoy, your strengths and your will. You have created your map through Steps 5, 6 and 7. Following this process you now know where you are and where you'd like to go. You've started taking consistent and considered action that you know is aligned to your goals and values (Step 8).

You're aware of the power of mind-set and are sufficiently tuned into yourself to know when you need to top-up your positivity or take more care of your overall wellbeing. Things feel fine and dandy – not much more to do, right?

Wrong. This is no time to be complacent or get too 'comfortable'. If you do, you run the risk of:

> Being unprepared for unexpected challenges and barriers that can still come your way; and

> Ignoring a quiet shift inside suggesting that actually, your destination now feels a little off course.

The first point is inevitable – we should expect challenges and prepare for them. The latter is not a problem *per se* but requires immediate attention.

Most people want things to be fairly simple. Our personal preferences dictate whether we prefer to follow a linear and clear process or a more fluid, responsive course of action. If the former, it's tempting to ignore possible obstacles as we push forward with our goals, milestones and action plans. This leaves us very vulnerable when things, invariably, don't follow the delineated and expected path. If we've got our head down and fail to look up now and again to check in with our progress, our feelings, intuition and the realities, we risk getting entrenched in a course of action that may not be taking us in the best direction.

As any sailor or hill walker knows, course correction is easier the sooner it's done. If a mistake has been made and you keep on in that direction, the distance to be crossed to rectify that mistake is far greater than if you'd done it sooner. Knowing our personal or behavioural preferences can be invaluable in this regard. On the Choose2Flourish Programme we apply the excellent 'C-me Profiling™ Tool that explores our preferences from three well recognised aspects of human personality:

> Task/ people focus;

> Reflective/ extravert; and

> Thinking/ feeling spectrum.

One simple way to check your bearings is to reflect and answer the questions provided in Steps 3 and 4 for the Flourishing Compass which are repeated below, along with a few additional points to consider.

How is this (course of action/ decision) serving your needs?

Will it take you closer to or further away, from where you want to be?

Are you doing what you enjoy?

Are you energised or depleted by what you are doing/ thinking of doing?

How are you using your strengths?

How motivated are you? What are you prepared to give up to ensure it happens?

How does this feed your purpose in the world?

Sometimes if we're open and trying to positively explore and respond to new opportunities, trying hard to 'go with the flow', we can feel overwhelmed by the amount of choices we have to make. We may get confused over where to spend our time and our ability to take decisions can be affected. This can lead us to exhaustion, despondency and low mood, shaking our confidence and self-belief. Slowing down, taking time to reflect (sleeping on it is always a good idea!) and using the 'head, heart, gut' check (see earlier steps) can help.

TIP: Create a habit of regularly checking in with yourself to explore how things are *really* going for you. Ask a trusted friend, partner or work with a professional coach to help you keep track of where you are going and how that matches where you think you'd like to be heading. Find 'accountability partners' who'll hold you to your commitments but also help you to explore your underlying motivations and desires.

Case Study: New Job = New Insights and Changing Career Priorities

Louise joined the Choose2Flourish Programme to help her transition into her new job. She was used to being the person driving the decisions and making things happen. However the new role was becoming very challenging as she could not longer 'get things done' in the manner and style she'd successfully used in the past. As a result, she was staying too late, working weekends and getting anxious about her impact and effectiveness. To top it all, she didn't think she was doing very well as a mother, making her feel guilty and inadequate.

Working through the process resulted in a number of 'Ah-ha's' for Louise. One was around her personal preferences and style of working. Being highly direct, challenging and task-orientated was fine in her previous role when she was actively line-managing people. Now that she needed to get things done by influencing rather than telling, it wasn't working. This was making her feel she had made a mistake with her new career direction but by stopping to examine what was really going on, she could see what needed to change and how she could adapt her leadership style.

Reflecting on how she was feeling and checking in with what was really important to her, she also realised the value she placed on being a 'good' mum. Understanding that helped her identify where and how she needed to change her priorities, empowering her to be more proactive in 'choosing to flourish' in her new role.

Step 10: Trust in Your New Beginning

Working through these steps will help you successfully make your way through the 3 stages of transition inherent in any career change, whether you are pro-actively leading this change or whether you are responding to external events beyond your control. Steps 1 and 2 are structured to help you with the 'endings' - what needs to be finished and let go of. You will find purposeful reflection and powerful insights emerging from the confusion of your time in the 'neutral zone'.

How quickly you move through the neutral zone is very much an individual matter, involving many factors such as personal circumstances, previous experience and the breadth and depth of the change you are seeking (e.g. a totally new purpose and direction in life or a promotion in the sector you're already committed to and happy within). How ready, willing and able you are to *adapt* also has an influence. After some point, however, you will be ready for your 'new beginning'. Of course, at this point you'll most likely ask yourself 'is this the real 'new beginning' or just a false start?'

Whilst it's going to be tempting, **make sure you do not force a new beginning before its time.** This can be difficult, especially where financial responsibilities are involved. Well meaning friends and family can also cause trouble here. When faced with conversations with someone seeking to leave their job or who has left their work, friends and family, somewhat naturally, want to know that you have a plan. That you are going to be okay. When people politely ask what you are going to do next, they're often not expecting (nor prepared for) an honest and real reply. For the recipient of such inquiries who is still deeply immersed in the uncertainty of it all, these questions can often be deeply frustrating (especially if the enquirer isn't prepared to really listen to the answer), as well as unsettling (especially if the recipient feels *expected* to know what they're doing).

It can be tempting, given the pressures we can feel or presume are being placed on us when we are in this situation, to grasp at anything that comes our way, if it even just feels vaguely 'right'. However it's so important to hold out until you've followed the previous steps and got yourself clear on the values, vision and balance you are seeking. You need to understand and own your strengths, to feel confident in your decisions. To becomes clear you have to use 'all of you', your emotions, your intuition as well as your reasoning, to know what you are now looking for.

The best way to 'know' a new beginning is how it *feels*. You should feel lighter, perhaps energized. Your physical body may respond in a positive way before your rational, logical brain has processed what has been going on. The path ahead will start to feel the right and only way. Granted, at the beginning, things will feel different – it's new, you are still adjusting. But inside there will be a sense that you are on the right path. People may comment on how you are looking – younger, thinner, refreshed. This will be reflecting the clarity and confidence that is growing inside you. Finally, when you are in sync with yourself, aligned to your purpose, values and strengths, there will be a **synergy** going on around you. The right people, opportunities, ideas will flow to you. Trust in the process and it will all come good.

Tip: You are on track when the new way starts to feel the right and only way. Whilst logic and working things through has it's place, ultimately the only way to judge whether you've found your 'new beginning' is whether or not it 'feels' right. The time spent tuning into your intuition as you've worked through the previous 9 Steps will help enormously here.

CHAPTER 6

Avoiding Common Pitfalls

Navigating a career change is invariably going to offer up challenges. These could be from both working through the internal transition and/or from the practicalities of managing the actual external change being contemplated. How can you even *think* about your next career move when you're exhausted at the end of the day by your current role and family responsibilities? When you yearn for something different but can see no way of achieving it, how do you find the motivation or techniques to think about things differently?

How much you have chosen and are in control of the change will be a strong influence over how you are likely to respond. Change that is created through no choice of your own, such as being re-deployed, being made redundant or having your role 're-imagined' (possible the worst euphuism for organisational driven change), is likely to create more negativity and resistance than if you're the one in the driving seat. It is, however, important to realise that even if you do feel you're the one in control, there may still be some internal resistance at work hindering your progress. We'll come on to this 'immunity to change' in a moment. First of all let's explore common fears that can sabotage our desire for taking our careers in a new direction. We'll then explore why expecting and preparing for *resistance* is a helpful perspective to take.

Illuminate the fears

One of my fears when I first started my latest career change, becoming a professional coach and creating my own business, was would I still be the same person? Would my family and my friends still relate to and love me if I became a very different person as a result of my inner journey? What would they think of me moving so far away from the qualifications, experience and career I had worked so hard for to follow my desire to be a coach and businesswoman? That fear made me procrastinate at first, made me doubt my path.

What I learned as I found my courage and built my confidence was that when you follow your path, when you align yourself and can be fully congruent with your strengths, your values, and your purpose, then the important people, well, they come with you! There's also the hidden benefit of bringing into your life all sorts of new and amazing people that now 'get' you. Those people become especially important as they support and understand the 'real' you that you are now allowing yourself to be.

Another common fear many express at the start of the Choose2Flourish Programme is that they don't believe that they can make money by following their heart, through realising their personal vision. This fear can run very deep and often, when you dig a little deeper, you realise that this may not even be *their* fear but that of their spouses, partners or parents. Limiting beliefs like this need to come into the open, to be challenged and questioned (as mentioned in Step 8). Often unquestioned assumptions lie at the heart of such beliefs. Challenging them, through seeking evidence and alternative perspectives, helps you see the reality, rather than accepting the false presumptions and the fear that generates. Whilst this statement may be somewhat overused, seeing 'fear' as the acronym for 'false expectations appearing real', is still helpful.

As we've mentioned in earlier chapters, what we think and believe creates neural pathways in the brain. Advances in the field of neuroscience have shown that our brains are in fact plastic; it is possible to re-wire your brain to think, believe and act differently. When you start to align yourself and take action congruent to who you want to be, and the goals you have for your life, new, unforeseen opportunities do come up. Having a new perspective, taking risks to try out new behaviour or ways of thinking means that fears can be overcome.

> **Case Study: Imposter syndrome sabotaging new leadership post**
>
> Outwardly Ann appears incredibly confident and successful. Appointed to a new job as principal in a large high school, Ann was hiding her insecurity. She didn't believe in her own abilities, despite such a visible vote of confidence in having secured such a high-powered, executive position. This lack of belief in herself was making her highly stressed and very anxious, which was impacting her family life and making her feel even worse.
>
> Through the programme we were able to help her understand how she was sabotaging herself. We explored the unhelpful thoughts, behaviours and habits she was using that were undermining her trust in herself. We rebuilt these into more empowering beliefs that translated into taking positive actions. She was guided into identifying and using her strengths, acknowledging the feedback that she was getting. By slowly seeking out evidence of her competency, Ann was able to manage her self-doubt and put into action a strong, aligned leadership style.

Manage Your Energy (and Your Time)

Probably the most common reason (or excuse) I hear from people on why they've not made that career change they've been talking about (in some cases, for years) is that they don't have the energy (quickly followed up by the additional excuse that they don't have the time). You need both, by the bucket-load, if you are serious about discovering a more fulfilling and flourishing path. So it might seem you're in a 'Catch-22' situation and no movement forwards can possibly be found. That will remain true for you unless of course you can tap into ways of managing your energy and re-prioritising your time.

Thinking back to Beckhard's Change Equation, change will only occur when you've got a motivating vision of the future, fully feel the pain of your current situation and can act on aligned, practical steps to move you forwards. This is a vitally important point for you to understand. If you don't feel the pain of where you are, you won't find the means to prioritise your time. Sometimes we need to really 'go there' to find that pain.

If you're not clear on what the procrastination, delay, lack of confidence and fear is **costing you right now**, as well as in the future, you've got to go looking! Likewise with **your vision**: It needs to sparkle, to have flesh on the bones, be illuminated in your mind's eye, drawn out, written down, read and looked at often. Once you have these two things clear, time management does become a lot easier to do. All the schedules, time mapping and diarising become wasted efforts if you're not clear on the 'why' pulling and pushing you forwards.

One of the very first things I realised when I shifted from being an employee into a businesswoman was that I needed to manage my energy. Regularly collapsing on the sofa after the children had gone to bed was not helping me do all the myriad of actions I needed to take in order to get my coaching business off the ground. That's when I started to pay very close attention to my 'N-PALS', to look at how I was using my brain during the day, and explore how I could be pro-active in supporting my performance by understanding what my brain needed. I also started to seek out different ways to managing my energy by researching various therapies and techniques that focus on the concept of the 'energy body'.

Every cell in our body vibrates with energy that flows through the Universe. Learning how to channel and amplify that, through Tai Chi or Qi Gong, for example, enables us to look after this vital aspect of ourselves. I opened myself up to this concept of the energy body through exploring a form of Qi Gong, which has now become a daily practice for me. This practice has been transformational in how

I've been able to manage my energy and juggle my day as a working mother, coach and businesswoman. Regular practices of mindfulness, meditation or yoga can have similar beneficial effects as we learn to switch off from the busy-ness of the world, slow down and retreat into a calm, rested state of mind instead. Find out what works for you. Adopt an experimental attitude and be open to trying out new things. A regular practice that calms you and works with your energy body is tremendously helpful for navigating a smoother path forwards in your career change and job search.

One very simple way of looking at this is to notice how you *feel* after being with different people, doing different things or being in certain situations or environments. Become aware of the impact these activities have on your energy levels. Doing more of what replenishes your energy and less of what drains you will empower you to have a more productive day. Working through the 10-Steps here requires you to allocate time and energy to doing it. Don't fall down on the 'no energy' hurdle that we can create for ourselves by not being aware of where we are 'wasting' our vital energy levels. Some people, as much as we might care for them, suck energy from us so we need to manage our exposure to that. You may find keeping an 'energy diary' will help you log what is going on and enable you to find different ways of keeping energised. Ask yourself, **Is what I'm about to do going to nourish or deplete my energy?**

Change and Other People

One aspect that often gets forgotten when considering change and how to transition into a new career or role is the effect this has on other people – and how their response to this affects you. In organisational change management, a common strategic model used to bring about change is Kotter's 8 stage Leading Change Model (2012). In Stage 2 of the model, considerable effort is placed on 'building the guiding coalition'. The same can be said for change at an individual level. You need supportive people around you with whom you can honestly discuss what is going on and explore options and possible actions. You need someone who can properly listen to you, help you explore your fears, and support you to find your solutions.

Finding your 'guiding coalition' may be easy for some – good friends, a trusted partner, an empathic parent. For others, this support may be less obvious but you still need to seek it out. Many on the Choose2Flourish Mastermind Programme have friends and family to talk with but enjoy the experience of sharing with others who are going through exactly the same kind of process, confusion and change in their careers. Others are very reliant on the coaching process and group, because rather than having a guiding coalition in their life they have the opposite – well-meaning but ultimately highly effective saboteurs!

As we explored in Chapter 4, social connection and a sense of belonging, is vital to our wellbeing. Feeling part of a community who share a similar identity can be very beneficial to us. However, if a member of that group starts to pull away, if they appear to be rejecting what that group stands for, that perceived rejection can be very difficult to handle for some. This can lead to resentment, antagonism and downright conflict in your relationships, at home, socially, as well as in work. This can be hard to deal with, especially if you're feeling more vulnerable than usual, so it's best having some insight into why people can react the way they do and how to deal with any resistance to the changes *you* are looking for.

In exploring your purpose in life, seeking to change your career direction, you are putting a mirror up to other people and asking them to examine their own life. The positive side to this is that it can mean you realise you've got your own mastermind group already surrounding you. I experienced this a few years ago when I realised that within my close friendship group there were two other women seeking considerable change in their career direction. This made for a real sense of camaraderie as we went about our respective new journeys – and for some excellent celebratory evenings when we acknowledged our triumphs!

On the flip side, however, even with well meaning friends, you may experience a range of less positive responses. These can include ignoring the issue (as asking you about what you're doing makes them feel very uncomfortable about their own situation), belittling your efforts or constantly telling you how difficult the job market is right now (or sharing other forms of their negativity and pessimism).

We spent some time at the start of this chapter looking at the possible fears that can hold people back from the career changes they seek. It's equally important to recognise in this process that in addition to dealing with your own fears, you may also experience and have to manage the impact of *other people's fear* around your career change. Other people can be very resistant to you changing career direction or seeking a new role for a variety of reasons. For example:

➤ They may not fully understand or value the reasons you provide for wanting change;

➤ They don't share (or agree with) the vision you've shared with them;

➤ They have come to different conclusions about what is lacking or missing for you;

➤ They have a low tolerance for change as a result of their personal preferences such as a higher need for security;

➤ They fear they are going to be left behind or become obsolete as you forge ahead on your new path;

➤ They can see something negative in what you are proposing which you are blind to seeing.

The last point is something to bear in mind. Those nearest and dearest to us often do understand us in a way we don't realise. Everyone has a blind spot where we can't appreciate certain aspects of our personality

CHOOSE TO FLOURISH: HOW TO CHANGE CAREER AND THRIVE IN LIFE

or attributes. If someone close to you is asking probing questions about some of your judgements and assumptions, listen carefully. You may want to ask some trusted friends and family for feedback around some of the areas you've explored in this guide.

How you manage resistance in others is very similar to how you might deal with resistance to change with an organisation. It's vital that you keep talking to them, sharing your honest thoughts and asking for their opinions. Involve them in your thinking and plans. Try to understand their concerns and be open to revising your thinking if what they say resonates or opens up new perspectives for you. A few more thoughts to consider here are:

- ➢ Most people don't respond well to shocks. If things aren't going well in work, if redundancy is on the cards or the frustration levels are rising, communicate well and often to ensure if you do resign or get made redundant, those close to you can have seen it coming;

- ➢ Seek first to understand then to be understood;

- ➢ Establish rapport first and be active in your listening to their concerns – we all know what it feels like when someone is *not* really listening to us!

- ➢ How well you communicate can be judged by the response you get back – which may be different from what you intended. Look at how you approached that conversation and try a different approach next time;

- ➢ You will always be communicating, even when you think you are not. A person cannot *not* communicate, and behaviour is the highest form of communication.

Being aware of the personal preferences of those people around you can be rather helpful here. People who are 'people focused reflectors'

('S' in the DISC model of behavioural profiling or 'Green' in the C-Me Profiling™ tool) have a tendency to be more resistant to change than extrovert, task focused types ('D' in the DISC model and 'Red' in the C-Me Profiling™ tool). Some people need a lot of facts, want to see all the detail and hear rational, logical explanations. ('C' in the DISC model and 'Blue' in the C-Me Profiling™). They won't respond very well to just your enthusiasm and flow of ideas, although that will be exactly what others need to hear from you ('I' types in the DISC model and 'Yellow' in the C-Me Profiling™). Adapting your communication to match the styles and needs of the person you are trying to reach out to will increase the success of that communication. Read up on behavioural profiling and experiment with how you explain yourself. You may be amazed at the shift in perspective and support you then get.

Immunity to Change: When You Can't Do What You Say You Will

When we seek to (re) discover purpose in our working life by pursuing a career change, we are compelled to integrate the rational, cognitive processing led by the **head**, with our emotions, our feelings, led by the **heart**, alongside taking action, led by the **hand**. When we are aligned with our passion and purpose, it would seem likely that we should be able to follow through on our commitments to make the necessary changes required to re-direct our path forwards. Sometimes, however, this is not the case and despite all best intentions, the goal setting or diary scheduling, we simply fail to engage the 'hand' to take action and we stagnate in our quest.

Take the following example from my client, Sarah. In realising the amount of self-reflection and research she needed to do, Sarah identified that getting up early in the morning was the best time to do it. She thought she could get up at 6 am and work on 'her stuff' for an hour before the rest of the family woke up. Time and time again, however, she would fail to do this. She'd go to bed too late and be too tired to get up early; or she wouldn't get out of bed even if she was awake. Sarah desperately wanted to change her job and could articulate all the reasons why she needed to go and what she was looking for. She'd worked through all her ten steps, or so she thought.

To help Sarah get past this impasse, we worked through the 'immunity to change' model devised by Robert Kegan and Lisa Laskow Lahey (2009). First Sarah listed what her commitment was in terms of her behaviour or 'improvement goal'. In this case, to get up early, by 6 am, so she could get to work on her career change actions (column 1 in the table below). We then worked through all the things she was doing/ not doing instead (column 2). Here we found Sarah was going to bed too late for a number of different reasons, not getting up early, and if she did get up, failing to get focused on her intended tasks and getting caught up in domestic chores instead.

1. Commitment	2. Doing/ Not doing instead
I commit to getting up early in the morning so that I can 'work on my stuff' around looking for a new career direction	Going to bed too late because I've been on Facebook & InstaGram responding to friends posts. I wait to eat dinner with Fred (husband) and it often gets really late once we've cooked together, eaten and cleared up. I'll wake up but stay in bed worrying about different things but not moving. I get up but go and sort out the washing or tidy and then the children are awake and I've lost my opportunity

The next step required Sarah to then consider what would concern or worry her the most if she tried to do the **opposite** to what she was doing in column 2. The answers here are where the biggest learning opportunity in the process often arises. Her answers immediately showed how there were two opposite and opposing drivers going on around her behaviour. Kegan describes this as having 'one foot on the gas, the other on the brake' when it comes to our progress in affecting change in our lives.

3. **Hidden competing commitments**
I need to hold a visible, central place in the lives of my friends. My marriage is important to me and it will suffer if I'm not making time for us to talk and be together. I need to feel a success, to get things right. I'd feel a failure if I do all this work and effort and nothing changes for me around my career. The house will fall into domestic chaos and that will be another thing I won't do very well. I'll stop being someone who's needed and important in my family. I won't be a good mum.

As you can see from the table above, all of a sudden we can now see the powerful counter arguments and deep seated fears Sarah has about her career change. Filling in this column gives her permission to say those things that up till now have been unsayable. By considering what assumptions underpinned these hidden commitments, (column 4) Sarah was able to see the real barriers behind being unable to set aside time each morning to work on her career goals.

4. **Big Assumptions**
Putting my career needs first will mean I'll lose my friends. The only way to ensure a good relationship with my husband is to make time to be with him over mealtimes every evening. It's my responsibility to make our marriage a success. I won't actually be able to find something I love and feel passionate about. I'm assuming I'm going to fail. I am the glue that keeps the house and family together. Good mums provide for all their children's needs.

When faced with the assumptions that Sarah was making, you can see why simply working on finding 'technical solutions' to the apparent problem was not going to work. As Kegan and Lahey (2009) say, what was required was an 'adaptive' solution whereby Sarah needed to 'evolve' her thinking and be able to step out of the 'hidden' commitments that 'held' her. By being able to now see the tension between her commitment and 'hidden commitments, she could instead find opportunities to test out assumptions instead. This creates a very different focus for action, involving an in depth look at the 'inner environment'.

Sharing Sarah's experience has hopefully given you an insight into the quality, depth and direction of thought that may be required if you find yourself unable to change a behaviour that needs to be changed! This has implications far beyond seeking a new career direction of course. (Anyone need to reach a healthy body weight?) Participants on the Choose2Flourish Mastermind Programme go through their own 'immunity to change' process, working on the 'one big thing' that's needed to help them make a success of their shift.

CHAPTER 7

Next Steps

Changing career direction, seeking out that new job that gets you leaping out of bed on a Monday morning does require effort and persistence. You need courage to overcome those fears, known and unknown; self-belief and confidence to seek out what it is you truly desire and to follow the path that inner reflection reveals. Responding to external changes, such as redundancy, that have happened to you rather than being led by you, requires *even more* from you in that regard. Understanding your transition is the essential key that unlocks the door to a smoother path to a new career that allows you to thrive.

You can expect to experience profound results and realise multiple benefits when this 10-step guide for successful transitions is followed. First of all, we start tuning in to our 'inner world' at a much deeper and more sensitive level. We become finely attuned to our 'inner voices', both the supportive and critical. The more self-aware we become, the more we are able to catch ourselves saying or doing things that aren't helpful or aligned to where we want to go or how we want to be. Internal criticism, which if left unchecked and unchallenged can sabotage our attempts at change, can be brought under control and managed. With persistence and effort, such inner views can be transformed. From that awareness, we can then start to shift into a state that says, "Well yes, perhaps. I can do this differently".

When you allow yourself to look at your life through a different lens, you start to see new opportunities that you simply did not believe would be there before. Some people can find this very hard to grasp at first, being so rigid in their viewpoints. This is why it is important to be open to new possibilities; to withstand a certain degree of uncertainty and *trust* in the process. Twenty odd years ago when I dreamed of being a published author, I had no way of knowing how I would get there, but I didn't let that stop me from retaining that dream. I kept myself open to that becoming a reality one day. 'Energy goes where your attention flows' is such a powerful statement. When you become aware of what you are focusing on, and make the conscious effort to focus on what it is you really want, rather than on what you *don't* want, things start to happen. As you allow yourself to grow, to move on through the process, you get clearer and more focused. You get a better handle on how you're prioritizing your time, where you're putting your energy. All of this combines to make the changes you seek more do-able, more manageable.

Another tangible result from following the Choose2Flourish approach to career change and transition is that it gets easier to make decisions. That is something that clients and participants on my programmes tell me again and again. Whereas before they procrastinated over what to do, how to do it and whether or not they should be doing it in the first place, after working through the Choose2Flourish approach, they get the clarity, conviction and confidence to decide. Things start to be done. This is especially true of those people who have really struggled in the past. They didn't have a clear vision. They didn't know what they wanted; only what they didn't want. By working through and trusting in the process, they start to get that missing personal vision. They start to get a purpose. That's where the magic really begins, because they then get the energy to do things differently, to move themselves forward, getting themselves unstuck.

If you don't know what you want, you're just going to stay in 'default mode'. You can stay hooked to that sat nav system with other people deciding what's coming to you. Choosing to flourish by contrast is all about being very proactive in the way you're making your choices, where you're spending your time, how you are thinking and behaving. All these things start to create a far fuller, and more meaningful, purposeful life. When you are able to follow the path that results in meaningful, happy and purposeful work, the effect of that ripples out around you.

Previous participants on my **Choose2Flourish Programme** delivered in in a VIP Intensive format describe the impact like this.

"Feeling stuck, fearful and frustrated, before attending this day I was unable to move on with my career goals. Now I realise it is easier to set smaller, achievable goals and challenges and I'm more confident and enthused. This was a very positive experience and I highly recommend the C2F VIP day – it was great knowing that others have struggled too".

Suzy Davies

"Before I came on the C2F VIP day I wasn't really sure why I was feeling so dissatisfied and unhappy in my role at work. Over the course of the day I discovered how being in transition affects you and that it is an important phase in change. Now I'm ready to start moving forward, from a place of acceptance and into the next phase of my life. Using the tools I learnt, I will be learning to 'live less in my head and more in my body' so that I can really tune into what I need. I highly recommend this programme as it changes the ways you think and feel about your current situation whatever stage you are at. Firm goals and actions for the future are established in a very personal way."

Judith Clancy

"I'd been feeling very uncertain, lacking in drive and energy to keep pushing forward in my current role. Over the course of the day with Rhian I've explored some of my barriers/ preferences and noticed that I am not operating effectively in many ways. I also clarified my desires and shifted on my future direction. Now I'm feeling clearer about immediate actions and am really excited about my future possibilities. I highly recommend this programme to anyone who wants to deepen their self-knowledge, find a way forward from a difficult situation or identify steps towards change or new possibilities."

Ian M

Tips and Hints

Following the 10-Step process outlined here will empower you to successfully make your transition into your next job or new career direction. At the very start, I said I wouldn't be covering the practicalities and 'best practice' involved in a job search, as the focus has been on supporting the internal transformation required to make a successful transition. However, I thought it would be useful to share a few strategies and tips to help spark off your own ideas for action. As with any 'top tip' list, you'll get better results if you come from, and use, your own particular suite of strengths and skills to shape your activity. There is no point picking a strategy that plumps you straight into your panic zone (e.g. cold calling).

➢ Identify people, on LinkedIn or in your network (include friends, their acquaintances, colleagues etc.) who are doing what you think you'd like to do. See what qualifications and experiences they have. Does this identify something you need to acquire (bearing in mind the next point)?

➢ Always be mindful that we tend to diminish what we have to offer and magnify the importance of what we see in others. Own your abilities; own your value.

➢ Before closing down to where you are now, as part of your 'what next?' journey, explore the possibilities of finding new meaning, purpose and accomplishment from staying put.

➢ The best way to find out whether you are suited to something you fancy doing is to **speak** with someone doing that role/ job. Find a way to be introduced to someone you think you should talk to (LinkedIn is great for this). Network outside of your work – network *inside* your place of work. Be aware that people, even the nicest, will need to know the "WIIFM' – what's in it for me? Successful people are busy. This might be common sense, but many people forget this: be respectful and make it easy for them to say yes to that 30-minute phone call or coffee.

➢ Make sure you are clear about *why* you are approaching them. Work out your objectives for the conversation but keep open to what they have to say.

➢ Successful networking is all about building relationships and reciprocity – what can you share, who do you know/ can introduce people to?

➢ Remember to keep breaking down your goals into small, manageable steps. Work with a professional coach if you find this difficult to do yourself. Don't shoot for the moon – aim for it but take aligned, purposeful action towards the sky first.

➢ Seek support; find your mentor, coach, fellow travellers and mastermind participants. Open up to your loved ones and share your dreams. No-one is expected to do this alone.

➢ Take yourself into places and situations where you can meet people who are in the sector you want to move into. Online groups are okay but even better are those that help you identify how to meet in person. MeetUp in the UK is good for this.

➢ Be very conscious of your personal brand – online and in person. What are you posting/tweeting/blogging about? Is it aligned to how you want yourself to be seen? Get feedback if you're not sure. People *always* check out possible applicants online. Use that to your best advantage.

➢ Persist but don't be a pest.

If you're reading this and have been stuck for sometime, now is the time to really ask yourself, 'what am I afraid of? What are my real fears here?' Write it all down. Create the space to quietly sit or go for a beautiful walk, be on your own, get out in nature. Try to listen to your heart. Give permission to yourself to explore your aspirations, hopes and dreams. If that feels a scary thing for you to do, tell yourself you're only looking, not acting at this moment in time. Opening the door doesn't necessarily mean you are going to walk through it. Remember when we put ourselves into our panic zone, we can't think clearly. We need to make it safe for us to move out of our comfort zone and into stretch. That's why working with a coach or with a group such as in my Choose2Flourish Mastermind Programme is so beneficial - we create that safe place for you to go exploring.

When I'm not sure what I should do, I use the 'head, heart, gut check' approach, which I think is very insightful and provides some profound answers that can help unstick you. It involves asking your head, heart and gut in turn, a question. If you're stuck in your transition and career move, these questions could be 'What's stopping me from moving on?' What am I afraid of?' or "What would help me the most right now?'

Listen to what your head tells you. It will tell you something quite logical, rational, such as "Oh, it's because I won't make any money". Ask your heart. The heart will tell you something different; it taps into your yearning, your emotional fears and hopes. Ask the same question to your gut. Often your gut will quietly tell you what's really going on. Use that insight to steer your course of action.

Your Invitation

We all have the ability within us to thrive. With work providing such a wonderful opportunity to find meaning, engagement, accomplishment, positive emotion and positive relationships (Seligman's 5 pillars to flourishing), it is a real loss, and comes at considerable cost, if we stop looking for something better. Following the 10 Steps outlined here will get you on your way – but you need the conviction, perseverance and courage to keep going. It can get challenging doing that all by yourself.

The Choose2Flourish Mastermind Programme, VIP Intensives and working privately with me all offer you essential on-going support, motivation and accountability, enabling you to flow smoothly through your career change. My invitation to you is to look carefully at how you can now empower yourself to keep moving forwards. Don't let reading this book be the last thing you do on this! Use the information contained here as a stepping-stone to realising what you fully need to flourish in your career and other aspects of your life. The one, final question you need to answer for yourself is this. **"What do you really need now to continue your journey?"** You've switched off the sat nav; you have your map and compass. Keep going brave explorer – it's a beautiful world out there.

Within the scale of the life of the cosmos a human life is no more than a tiny blip. Each one of us is a visitor to this planet. A guest, who has only a finite time to shine. What greater folly could there be than to spend this short time lonely, unhappy, in conflict with our fellow visitors? Far better surely, to use our short time in pursing a meaningful life, enriched by a connection with and in service toward others.

Dalai Lama

"Being you is the quickest way to true, sustained success. When you know what you want and find the courage to go after it, you are truly alive."

Rhian Sherrington

Choose2Flourish Ltd
Canningford House
1st Floor
38 Victoria Street
Bristol
BS1 6BY
Rhian@choose2flourish.co.uk

www.choose2flourish.co.uk

Resources

Bach, R. (1972) *Jonathan Livingston Seagull*, Pan Books

Beckhard, R. & Harris, R. T. (1987) *Organizational Transitions: Managing Complex Change*, 2nd Edition, Pearson Education Inc

Brann, A. (2015) *Neuroscience for Coaches: How to Use The Latest Insights For The Benefit Of Your Clients*, Kogan Page

Bridges, W. (2004) *Transitions: Making Sense of Life's Changes*, Da Cao press, 2nd Edition

Brown, B. (2012) *Daring Greatly: How The Courage To Be Vulnerable Transforms The Way We Live, Love, Parent And Lead*, Penguin Group

Chopra, D. & Tanzi, R.E. (2013) *Super Brain: Unleash the Explosive Power of Your Mind*, Random House

Coelho, P. (1988) *The Alchemist*, Harper Collins Publishers

Covey, S.R. (2004) *The 7 Habits of Highly Effective People: Powerful Lessons in Personal Change*, Simon & Schuster UK Ltd

Fredrickson, B.L. (2008) *Positivity*, Three Rivers Press

HH Dalai Lama & Culter, H.C. (1998) *The Art of Happiness: A Handbook For Living*, Hodder & Stoughton

Hill, N. (2007), *Think And Grow Rich*, Wilder Publications

Huffington, A. (2014*) Thrive,* WH Allen

Kegan, R. & Lahey, L.L. (2009) *Immunity to Change: How to Overcome it and Unlock The Potential In Yourself And Your Organization,* Harvard Business Press

Kotter, J.P. (2012) *Leading Change*, Harvard Business Review Press

Kotter, J.P. & Rathgeber, H. (2006) *Our Iceberg Is Melting: Changing and Succeeding Under Any Conditions*, MacMillan

Maslow, A. H. (1954). *Motivation and Personality*, Harper and Row

Maslow, A. H. (1943). A Theory of Human Motivation. *Psychological Review, 50(4)*, 370-96.

Rock, D. & Page, L.J. (2009) *Coaching With The Brain In Mind*, Wiley

Seligman, M. (2011) *Flourish: A New Understanding of Happiness and Well-Being and How To Achieve Them*, Nicholas Brealey Publishing

Sherrington, R. (2014) *Alchemy for the Mind: Create Your Confident Core*, Practical Inspiration Publishing

Tay, L., & Diener, E. (2011) Needs and subjective well-being around the world. *Journal of Personality and Social Psychology, 101(2)*, 354

Tracy, B. (2010) *Goals! How To Get Everything You Want – Faster Than You Ever Thought Possible*, Berrett-Koehler Publishers, 2nd Edition

Printed in Great Britain
by Amazon